Living with
Limericks

Garrison Keillor

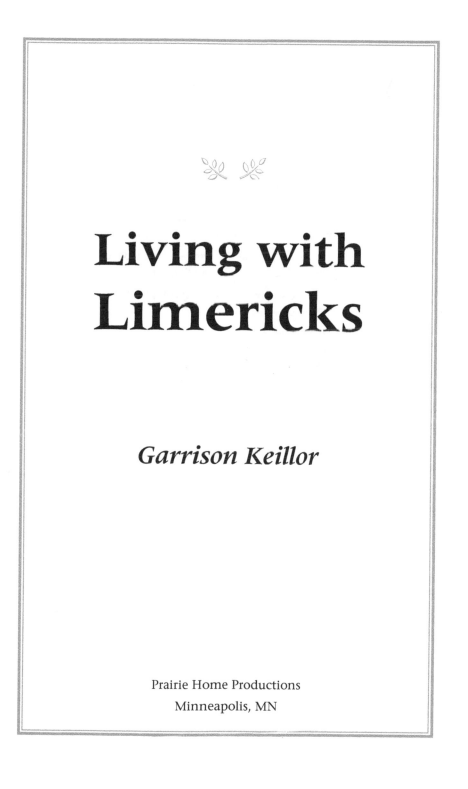

Living with Limericks

Garrison Keillor

Prairie Home Productions
Minneapolis, MN

Published in the United States by Prairie Home Productions,
Minneapolis, Minnesota. GarrisonKeillor.com

Library of Congress Control Number: 2019914470
Paperback ISBN-13: 978-1-7330745-1-3
Publication Date: November 15, 2019
First Edition

Cover image: Garrison Keillor
Cover design, interior design, and composition:
Leigh McLellan Design

To the memory of Frederick Keillor, 2000–2017,
who would've studied this book, then gone off
and written thirty or forty originals about small
mammals, automobiles, the firmament of
heaven, and multifarious friends.

There was an old man of Anoka
Who one day wrote (as a joke) a
Humorous verse
That turned into a curse
Like a twitch or compulsion to polka.

His obsession appeared to increase
As they tried to get him to cease.
His family pleaded:
"No more limericks needed!"
And then—his great masterpiece!

He wrote "There was" and stopped short
And started to snicker and snort
And convulsed in laughter
Went to the Hereafter
And so said the coroner's report:

"Violent laughter's the cause
Of death. I grieve for your loss."
So they put him down
In a hole in the ground
And the tombstone said simply: "There was."

Also by Garrison Keillor

Poetry

O, What a Luxury

77 Love Sonnets

Lake Wobegon

Lake Wobegon Days

Leaving Home

We Are Still Married

Wobegon Boy

Lake Wobegon Summer 1956

In Search of Lake Wobegon

Pontoon

Liberty

Pilgrims

Other Works

Guy Noir and the Straight Skinny

A Christmas Blizzard

Daddy's Girl

Homegrown Democrat:
A Few Plain Thoughts from the Heart of America

Love Me

Me, by Jimmy "Big Boy" Valente

The Sandy Bottom Orchestra (w. Jenny Lind Nilsson)

The Book of Guys

WLT: A Radio Romance

Happy to Be Here

Contents

⚕ 1 ⚕

From Whence It Came

IT IS A SIMPLE but elegant form, five lines, rhymed, sprung from a guy named Anon two or three or four hundred years ago, a little dance familiar to every literate person, though sometimes with a trick ending.

> There was an old man of Nantucket
> Who died. He just kicked the bucket.
> And when he was dead,
> They found that instead
> Of Nantucket he came from Barnstable.

I am the old man of Anoka and at the age of 77 I look back on a life that was affected by compulsive limericizing. How does it happen? One of the first things I did after meeting my wife in the spring of 1992 and falling in love with her over lunch was to write her a limerick.

> I'm suddenly crazy for Jenny
> Whose virtues are lustrous and many.
> Her faults are few,
> One, maybe two,
> Though right now I can't think of any.

And when our daughter came along and learned to read, I wrote one for her.

> A beautiful child named Maia
>
> Decided she must satisfy a
>
> Wonderful urge
>
> To run into church
>
> And cry, "Hallelujah! Hey! Hiya!"

I went into a limerick frenzy once on tour in Washington State, looking at a map and before long I'd written:

> A young fellow from Walla Walla
>
> Found Christian faith too hard to falla
>
> And do what Christ says
>
> So he put on a fez
>
> And is happier following Allah.

> A lady who lived in Vancouver
>
> Drank two quarts of varnish remover
>
> And did not get ill
>
> And vomit, but still,
>
> It didn't do much to improve her.

> A lady who lives in Seattle
>
> Will not eat fish, fowl, or cattle.
>
> No meat, blood, or bone,
>
> Or greens that were grown
>
> On or near the site of a battle.

> One Halloween in Wenatchee,
>
> A man dressed as an Apache,
>
> Painted, tattooed,
>
> Perfectly nude,
>
> For the breechcloth was simply too scratchy.

A powerful girl of Puyallup
Waits for her lover to call up
And say he'll be late,
Then she stands by the gate
And decks him with one mighty wallop.

One after another, I became the unacknowledged limerick laureate of Washington. My life at that point was much too disciplined: the radio show was popular, my novel *Pontoon* was on the bestseller list ("a tough-minded book…full of wistfulness and futility yet somehow spangled with hope" —*New York Times*), I was writing another and also a screenplay, but what moved me more deeply was the challenge of writing pointless limericks. I discovered that the L in Snoqualmie is silent and I whipped off a good one.

A gentleman lived in Snoqualmie
Who was fond of cheese and salami
Though they gave him gas
And whenever he'd pass,
There was wind, sometimes a tsunami.

Frankly, I was out of my mind.

There was an old fellow of Bellingham
So stubborn that there was no telling him.
His wife said, "My dear,
I wish you weren't here."
He ignored her and she wound up selling him.

A young man climbed Mount Rainier
On a day that was perfectly clear.
He reached the summit,
Looked down and, dadgummit,
Saw his car and his wife disappear.

A young fellow left Puget Sound
To move to Spokane and he found
That he hated blue sky
And the air was too dry
And the coffee improperly ground.

And finally, on a ferryboat heading for Seattle from Bainbridge Island:

The captain cried out to the purser:
"Help me! I cannot reverse her."
He had programmed
The boat and it rammed
The dock—he could not find the cursor.

And I came home to Minneapolis, and felt obliged to write:

Minneapolis is great. Have you seen it?
The streets go from Aldrich to Zenith.
It's the birthplace of Prince,
Than whom no one since
Has been any hipper, I mean it.
The city is good for the sickly.
The streets are numerical, strictly,
And alphabetical
All so that medical
Teams can get to you quickly.

I come from a Christian home with a piano where my mother played "Jesus, lover of my soul, let me to Thy bosom fly while the nearer waters roll, while the tempest still is nigh," which I still love to sing in company with others, but life is disorderly and we don't march in straight lines and when I was in grade school I heard boys on the playground singing a GI ditty of World War II and the rhythm of the words appealed to me. It was a limerick: *Hitler had just one ball. Goebbels had two but they were small. Himmler had something simmler and Goering had no balls at all.* Vulgarity serving the Allied war effort, patriotic but it had to be transmitted from boy to boy, avoiding informants, i.e., girls. What appealed to me was the gracefulness of the form wrapped around the degradation, like gilded dog turds on linen doilies.

In the Keillor household, testicles were never mentioned. Bodily functions were studiously ignored; at the dinner table, a fart passed without comment. Our words for elimination were "No. 1" and "No. 2" but generally, we just said, "Go to the bathroom"; even if you did it in the woods, you still "went to the bathroom." Our decorous manners had a spiritual underpinning—"Would Jesus want to hear you talk like that?" my mother said, when she heard me use the word "shitty." I was trying it out and she slapped it down. She erected a high fence against obscenity and profanity, so that when I was in the eighth grade and found, in the Anoka High School library, on the open shelves, within sight of Miss Goodner at her high pulpit of a circulation desk, a volume of unexpurgated limericks collected by Gershon Legman, I simply went to pieces. I read about the *young couple from Aberystwyth who united the parts that they kissed with and then in their passion, after a fashion, they united the parts that they pissed with* and I experienced violent involuntary convulsive laughter, my face turned to rubber, belly heaving, and when I read *There was a young couple named Kelly who were found lying belly to belly because in their haste they used library paste instead of petroleum jelly,* snot ran out of my nose, I sat snorting and whinnying, and then the limerick that killed me, the one about *the young man of Madras whose balls were made out of brass—he clanged them together to play "Stormy Weather" as lightning came out of his ass.* It was a transforming ecstatic experience.

The women I know never had that experience. They grew up in liberal-minded homes in which testes and sexual intercourse were talked about, whenever necessary, in an open and reasonable way based on factual information gained from reputable sex hygiene books and so the limericks are not funny but simply absurd.

I passed *the young man of Madras* around geometry class at Anoka High School and heard stifled snickers—and the teacher grabbed the paper and read it and did not laugh. He said to me, "You are the last person I would've expected that from." I didn't want to be the first person he'd expect it from, but I didn't care to be last either. It was a great limerick. The part about "Stormy Weather" played by musical testicles was inspired but it was the lightning that made the poem truly great. You could have had broccoli come out of his ass, or nickels, or window shades, but lightning was what raised the thing to the level of Wagner or Raphael. It takes a strict religious upbringing to respond fully to that limerick, and my mother, Grace, laid the foundation for what has now become a lifelong occupation.

> My mother whom I adored
> Is in heaven where, with one accord,
> Saints clang their balls
> In heavenly halls
> As they fall on their knees to the Lord.

I am 77 and I am still engaged with the form that entranced me as a third-grader. This is embarrassing, of course, but I've learned to live with it. My brother Philip did extensive research on shoreline erosion on Lake Michigan and my sister Judy taught third grade, my brother Steven is a historian and brother Stan is an attorney, and sister Linda has raised money for a series of nonprofits.

> The fundraiser Linda Joanne
> In service to woman and man
> Raised buckets of dough
> To endow and bestow,
> Donate, bequest,
> Empower, invest,
> To finish what others began.

My cousin Dr. Dan became a man of science, with wide-ranging interests in biology, meteorology, botany, geology, and, of course, medicine.

The diligent internist Dan
Is stuck with being the man
To urge compliance
With medical science
Which you won't though you should and you can.

My cousin Elizabeth, the smartest person in the family, earned a doctorate in psychology.

The argumentative Betty
Has an intellect ever ready
To critique the phoni-
Ness of macaroni
Compared to the truth of spaghetti.

Relatives have succeeded in architecture, astrophysics, information technology, organic farming, history, engineering, fundraising for nonprofits, and what have I done to make this world a better place? I wrote:

The young fellow answered an ad
And was hired and cried, "I'm so glad
To be given this chance
I could pee in my pants"
And we looked and saw that he had.

My excuse is my very low threshold of boredom. There are more and more empty lulls in life and they seem to get longer and longer such as right now as I sit two thousand miles east of New York and write:

I sit on a ship on the sea
And experience infinity
With nothing to do
But look up at you
While you stand staring at me.

> Here I sit, amusing myself,
> Past the spot on the Atlantic shelf
> Where, anguished and frantic,
> The good ship Titanic
> Went down in nineteen-and-twelve.

I'm on the *Queen Mary 2*, eastbound from New York to Southampton, and Jenny and I sit in deck chairs drinking tea and looking out at the watery horizon in all directions, she reading a thrilling novel and I writing an adventure limerick.

> A U-boat appears to starboard
> And fires a torpedo toward
> Our ship where I stand,
> A pistol in hand,
> In the other a bright silver sword.

> "You missed, you cowards!" I cry.
> "Show your faces and die!"
> I swear at the Nazi
> And fire two shots, he
> Falls, looking up at the sky.
> The U-boat sinks
> And a waiter brings drinks,
> A martini for me, very dry,
> And I look at you,
> The lady in blue,
> As you smile and give me the eye.

Ever since childhood, the limerick has appealed to me, the vulgarity of course, but also the tidiness and concision, like a jewel box of English. Perfection is rare in real life but it is possible to write a perfect limerick. I wrote a string of my own in high school, most of them fairly conventional, and others not bad:

There was a young writer named Gary
Who grew up out on the prairie
Among Christian folks
Who never told jokes
Or swore, even when necessary.

Scripture says, Love one another
And treat every man as your brother.
Therefore, mister,
Each woman's your sister,
So don't make her into a mother.

I wrote them in a small precise hand in a notebook and was surprised at how the rhymes and the form led me off in a racy direction. I showed them to nobody.

We were solid Plymouth Brethren, evangelical fundamentalist folks, and I had never heard the word "unexpurgated" before—we lived in a state of perpetual expurgation—and this religious underpinning made me susceptible. Rock and roll was founded by young men who'd learned to whoop and yell for the Lord and then fell off the evangelical wagon. My inherited rectitude drove me to vulgar limericks.

I first recited a limerick in public in Lavona Person's ninth-grade speech class. A painful three minutes for a shy person with much to be self-conscious about. I was 6 feet tall, weighed 138, wore half-rim horn-rimmed glasses, hand-me-down (from my sister) high-water pants that zipped up the side, size 10 shoes, and a home haircut, long on top, shaved around the sides, like Kim Jong-un's. I couldn't play sports because I had a heart valve problem, couldn't do after-school activities because I was a bus kid from out in the sticks, not allowed to hitchhike. I was easily distracted and my industrial arts teacher, Mr. Orville Buehler, found it terrifying to watch me solder or use a jigsaw, he imagined I'd immolate myself or cut off a hand, so he sent me upstairs to Miss Person and my first assignment was Oral Interpretation and I chose to do limericks. As a warm-up, I recited two by Anon—*There was a young lady of Sheba to whose bed there came an amoeba, this absurd piece of jelly crawled up on her belly and cried out in rapture, "Ich liebe."* And *There was an old man of Khartoum who was filled with sorrow and gloom and anxiety in 1893 and now he is dead, I presume.*

And then:

> There was a young man of Anoka
> Who tried to write a great limerick.
> He tried and he tried
> And some were not bad,
> But something seemed to be missing.

Miss Person laughed. Corinne Guntzel, the smartest girl in the class, laughed, and then the rest of the class, assured that it was indeed funny, laughed, and that one limerick elevated me (briefly) to be one of the cool kids. I had written a joke and it was a good one.

Writing poetry was an easy way to get attention: nobody else did it except a few girls and their poems were along the lines of *If only we would open our hearts to beauty, there would be no more hatred or war,* which is thin soup compared to *There was a young couple of Aberystwyth.* Limericks could be wild and the meter and rhyme gave them the appearance of decorum. A beautiful combination. I didn't care for serious poetry in school: it seemed full of falsehoods. Love is definitely not the star to every wandering bark, and April is not the cruelest month, March is. The best minds of our generation are not starving, hysterical, naked—most of them are well fed, calm, and very well dressed, thank you. Robert Frost's little horse was right: it is queer to stop without a farmhouse near, the darkest evening of the year.

I was a very ordinary oddball—skinny, nearsighted, bookish, tongue-tied, no evidence of brilliance whatsoever—and limericks were an escape from self-consciousness. They weren't about me. The first suggestive limerick I wrote was—

> A young fellow from Brooklyn Park
> Liked to park with a girl in the dark
> And what they did

> In the car where they hid
> Is not found in the Gospel of Mark.

I showed it to a girl I knew and she was alarmed. "Why do you write dirty verse?" she said. "It's so immature." It was 1960, in Anoka people were on the alert for oddity, and I did not wish to bring shame to the family. Still, it was thrilling to write surreptitiously.

> A Catholic sister passed gas
> While she sat by the window, alas,
> At Saturday Mass
> And it stained the glass
> With a photograph of Balaam's ass.

In English class, we were reading about Richard Cory who put a bullet through his head even though he was nicely dressed and had nice manners—an utterly stupid poem; and the dope who stopped by the woods on a winter evening and watched the snow fall—what's the point??; and that dreary mopefest about J. Alfred Prufrock and whether or not he dares to eat a peach or wear his trousers rolled. I knew in my heart that the young man of Madras was superior to all of them. And the laughter in Miss Person's speech class was an enormous moment I remembered for years afterward, an awkward kid with glasses and all of that good feeling directed his way.

Success at the age of fourteen. My life saved by Miss Person in her ruffled white blouse, her green plaid wool skirt, her knee socks and loafers, fresh out of Augsburg College, standing in the back of the room and laughing harder than anyone. Many years later, I told the story at her retirement dinner, and she beamed, and ten years after that, at her memorial service. The school is on Second Avenue in Anoka. I know which room was hers, and one of these days I might go put a bronze plaque on the wall:

> Lavona, the day you stood here
> And your laughter rang loud and clear
> At the limerick I wrote,

You launched my boat
And gave me, my dear, a career.

Everything starts from somewhere.
A scratch of the match lights the flare.
They laughed, you guffawed,
And thanks be to God,
I went and told jokes on the air.

2

A Young Man Tried to Distinguish Himself with a Major in English

Here is a yawp for old Walt
Whitman, who's well worth his salt
Though sometimes he'll slip
And just let her rip
And say, "Camerados! What is this blade of grass?
Who am I? Who are you" And you have to say, HALT.

I SET LIMERICKS aside in college so I could try on the available intellectual pretensions and learn to affect ambiguity, writing fractured verse, darkly incomprehensible, for the student literary magazine, *The Ivory Tower*, whose readers would have relished what Shakespeare's crowd wanted— unsparing exposure of despicable men, blood and gore, comely heroines, raucous comedy, and instead we gave them unhappy soliloquies by lonely outsiders.

Birch boughs reach out like ghosts
In the dark woods where nobody waits for me
Or cares that my head hurts.
The telephone wires
Vibrate with pointless conversation. Why am I
Drifting in this dark boat? The owl with the broken
Wing flies through the moonless night—

He does not know his entire family is
Gone, the nest fallen, beautiful feathers scattered
On the ground like snowflakes.

We were writing, not in service to readers but to impress each other with our implacable bleakness, which we did not actually feel, only imagined, as you'd imagine what you might say if you suffered from schizophrenia and then said it.

Why did I write so obscurely?
I knew it was devious, surely.
It's sad, years later,
To be the creator
Of writing that travels so poorly.

Meanwhile I earned my way through school as a dishwasher, a parking lot attendant, and a YMCA camp counselor, an English major with no lifesaving skills taking children on canoe trips into the Boundary Waters, feeding them freeze-dried food that turned to stone in our bowels.

I do not like camping at all,
Not winter, spring, summer, or fall.
I hate snakes and owls
And can't move my bowels
Except in a warm toilet stall.

I was set on becoming a writer. We had poets around, available for imitation. I liked Allen Tate, a kind man who brought a bottle of Scotch to his poetry seminar and shared it with us.

Allen Tate was distinguished and old
And had written an ode (rather cold)
To Confederate dead
Which no one had read
But it was great, we were told.

I took a humanities course from James Wright, a good man who was going through a rough period, and in class at 8 a.m. at a lectern in Folwell Hall, he looked hungover and heartbroken as he lectured on Dickens's *Hard Times*. I admired Wright's poems and I felt that, if being hungover and heartbroken and lecturing to indifferent sophomores at 8 a.m. was how you got to be a fine poet, I'd rather not, thank you very much.

> The humanities teacher James Wright,
> Hungover from Saturday night,
> Stared at his class,
> Deep in his morass,
> Like a Camel in search of a light.

> I learned his poems verbatim
> And gave myself one ultimatum:
> The alcohol breath,
> The eyes full of death,
> I vowed I would not imitate him.

And then there was John Berryman, a brilliant man who, at his poetry readings, packed with admirers, was completely shit-faced, his speech slurred, muttering private non sequiturs to friends in the audience. He leaped to his death from the Washington Avenue Bridge one cold winter day in 1972. When I heard of his death, I quit writing poetry entirely and switched to verse. If you know you're not going to jump off the bridge, why call for help?

> The tortured poet John Berryman
> Was a strange, alcoholic, and scary man.
> He might've been stronger
> And lived a lot longer
> Had he been a truck driver or dairyman.

> At age fifty-seven, old John
> Jumped from a bridge, landing on

A yard full of coal.

God rest his soul.

He made a small hole, now he's gone.

Another model was Robert Bly, who lived on his boyhood farm in western Minnesota, an oracular man who liked to speak large inspired things suddenly out of nowhere: *"The highway does not go where we think it goes!"* You hesitate to ride in a car with a man like that for fear he might steer into a cornfield following the flight of a crow. But he was hardworking, generous, and as a good Lutheran he avoided the greasy fingers of alcohol and unreasonable despair.

> Every day around dawn Robert Bly
>
> Writes a poem, that is no lie,
>
> And the poem he composes
>
> At the end of his nose is
>
> Looking him straight in the eye.
>
> And with great clarity
>
> Addresses posterity
>
> Though he is not intending to die.

Allen Ginsberg came to campus once and gave a reading to a few hundred people. He sat cross-legged on the stage, in a white gown, making a few chords on a harmonium, chanting his poems. Allen believed in First Thought Best Thought and never edited himself and as the reading went on, I realized that the poems would've meant more to people who didn't understand English. He was not one of the best minds of his generation. He was a sweet man, but after a while you were grateful to have come late and found a seat in back and could step quietly away and go have a beer.

> Ginsberg was ruined by fame.
>
> His howls became much the same
>
> When he made a decision
>
> To give up revision.
>
> Now he's unknown except for his name.

Some students I knew went in for haiku, which struck me as emaciated and ungenerous, but for a while they appeared in every little literary magazine.

> The black night descends
> And I am out of Pall Malls
> As I wait for death.

I never committed a haiku, not even in secret. I once shoplifted a book from a bookstore, I lied in order to escape from social engagements, I once stopped on a walk and stared at a window where a woman was walking wet and naked to get a towel out of a closet, but I never wrote a haiku. Never felt the need to impersonate mysticism. Haiku were beyond criticism. A friend showed you his haiku, you were obliged to look at them with respect and say, "I like that" or words to that effect.

> The bare trees are like
> Dead fingers, a frozen sea
> Fills my whole being.

Extreme reticence posing as art, but it was taken seriously, while the limerick was scorned, though it takes some craft and cunning to fashion a good one. Anyway, in Minnesota the frozen sea is outdoors, not within you, and it isn't a sea, it's a lake. And the haiku quickly disappeared in the big wind of counterculture that blew in from the West around 1969/70, people my age practicing serious playfulness, making long flowing Whitmanesque poetry and instantaneous art, twirling on the grass with girls named Meadow and Saffron.

> Back in the Sixties I dressed
> In a flowery shirt and bright vest,
> Big boots and red socks
> And long flowing locks,
> A medieval man in the Midwest.
>
> We lived in perpetual awe
> On refreshments forbidden by law,

Giddy and naked
We jumped in the lake at
Midnight to shock the bourgeois.

It was all very exciting, the marching and manifestos, the brave protest songs never heard by those they were intended for, the booming rhetoric and draft-card burning, hippie encampments and caravans, the hip urbanites on a quest to become innocent rustics, and a ludicrous outfit called Poets Against The War, flocks of poets writing bad anti-war poems and feeling highly righteous in front of small crowds who felt obligated to clap and cheer for a show that had less political effect than a light afternoon drizzle, everywhere you looked you saw people admiring themselves for righteous resistance that consisted of carrying a sign. I know. I was there. I was one of them. And it all came to nothing except the election of Richard Nixon in 1968 and the perpetuation of the war in Vietnam past all limits of reason and decency and the deaths of a million more people, and Nixon, guilty of perpetuating pointless carnage, was eventually shamed for trying to cover up a minor burglary in which nobody so much as sprained an ankle.

Nixon was a desperate crook
At whom history will throw the book
Just for the war
He was on the hook for
Prolonging and the lives that it took.
A classic schlump and a schnook,
He should've been hung on a hook
And shown no mercy
But he moved to New Jersey,
Forsaken (or is it forsook?).

The "movement," as people called it, was play-acting, self-absorbed, a crowd in a reefer haze on a hillside stupefied by three hours of very loud bad music, and our writing that came out of the era is embarrassing.

> And now it's fifty years later
> And our poetry needs a translator.
> What was psychedelic,
> Holy, angelic,
> Is an odd little relic,
> An adding machine calculator.

I wore a hippy shirt and let my hair grow down over the collar but mainly I tried to focus my consciousness, not expand it. I had my mind set on writing humor for *The New Yorker*. It paid real money, it was read by people I admired who I wished would admire me, and I believed that publication in it might lead to other things. So I didn't get tangled up with drugs. The friend who tried to introduce me to coke was a photographer and a poet who felt it unleashed her creative energies. She died at fifty-two, leaving behind shoeboxes full of blurry photos, mostly shot from moving cars: they were about the act of photography rather than making strong pictures. Her poems were bundles of scraps. I was asked to speak at her memorial and I declined. What I had to say shouldn't be said to weeping people.

> A young poet out on the prairie
> Took pills to feel extraordinary,
> Did opium, speed,
> Smoked bundles of weed,
> Drank absinthe, cognac, and sherry.
>
> The effect was astonishing. Very.
> She wrote so much it was scary.
> And then by and by
> She asked herself, "Why
> Am I lying in this mortuary?"
>
> Her friends assembled to carry
> The urn to the town cemetery,
> A gust of wind blew,

And her ashes all flew,

Leaving nothing of Cherie to bury.

Her memory was kept

By the sexton who swept

Up the dust. God heal

Our souls. He is real

And now she is imaginary.

My teachers urged us toward serious literature that grappled with man's fate, and I preferred comic literature in which man grappled with the lid of a jar of pickles. I forswore ambiguity. I liked Schiller's *Mit Freude, die uns Kunst bereitet, Entlohnt uns Gott für seine Willkür.*

The pleasure that art can afford us

Is reward for life's cruelty toward us,

Strangers in a foreign land,

Floating on a grain of sand.

To amuse, as best it can,

Is the gift of art to man.

In German literature, the limerick was almost nonexistent until Schiller's son Fred wrote one during the year he taught German at Carleton College in Northfield, Minnesota.

Schwer zu Papier ist Deutsch gebracht,

Es wird dabei nicht leicht gelacht,

Will ich unterhalten,

Muß ich auf Englisch walten,

Und—logisch—auf Französisch in der Nacht.

German is so hard to write

And make sound airy and light

And so when I wish

To amuse, it's English,

And naturally French late at night.

I heard about Schiller from Bill Holm who lived at the end of a straight stretch of county road extending a hundred miles west of Minneapolis to the town of Minneota and his old house full of books and harpsichords. I liked to drive out and listen to him declaim on the sad state of American culture and the history of his Icelander family. He claimed not to be a believer but he played organ often in the local Lutheran church and he knew a good deal of Scripture by heart. He adored Whitman and I did not.

> Bill Holm was a joyful Icelander,
> Who delighted in stories with candor
> And he loved to meet us
> Through Bach partitas,
> And the preludes and fugues, even grander.
> He sat at his old harpsichord
> As the music was leading him toward
> A gravestone in
> The midst of his kin
> And a meeting, at last, with the Lord.

He died at sixty-five, of pneumonia, returning home from Arizona one cold February, having stoutly resisted the pleas of friends to stop smoking, drink less, and reduce his intake of animal fats. Three years before, he had been a big hit at a live *PHC* broadcast from Reykjavik. An Icelandic men's chorus was on that show and Bill was transported by the solemn grandeur of their voices. He read a poem about his mother, Jona, and declaimed about old Icelanders he had grown up with and afterward he and I drove out to a white house at the end of a long road by the sea and knocked on the door, which was opened by Ólafur Ragnar Grimsson, the president of Iceland, himself, no security man in sight, and we went in to dinner. The drinking was prodigious.

One night, a few years later, sobered by Bill's death, I quit drinking. I read a book from A.A. about the twelve-step program and it sounded pretty dreadful, sitting in a circle of folding chairs in a church basement talking about our emotionally distant fathers. I dreaded the idea of group therapy and to avoid it, I stopped drinking. Not a problem.

It's easier than people think
To be sober and not take a drink.
Just say, O screw it.
And then do not do it,
It's simpler than calling a shrink.

3

Returning to Form

ALL THROUGH MY teens and twenties, I looked forward to getting older. Teenagehood was celebrated in the 1950s but not by me. I didn't do the Twist, didn't have a ducktail or wear saddle shoes, didn't hang out at the drive-in. I wanted to grow up.

> Youth is a fabulous pill—
> Instilling the thrill of free will
> And crazed liberty—
> And, fortunately,
> A prescription one cannot refill.

After graduation I hung around the U because, when someone asked what I was doing, it felt good to say, "I'm in grad school." But as the Sixties ended, I married, a child was born, I needed to earn a living, so I turned to prose fiction and radio comedy. I did an early morning radio show in Minnesota and *The New Yorker* bought a story of mine, and then another and another. I was twenty-seven. Bill Kling was my boss, Roger Angell was my editor in New York, both of them generous and friendly, their appreciation wholehearted and their criticisms tinged with regret, so I had an easier road than anyone else I knew.

I escaped from the solemn (*Ahem*)
English Department (bless them)
And did radio
Divertimento
Six days a week, 6 a.m.

At dawn in dim light, all alone,
I sat at a small microphone
And spoke to the dark
Of life's trailer park
In a comical intimate tone.

Came home to my black Underwood
And wrote and rewrote as one should
And rewrote again,
Proofread it, and then
Sent it off in hopes it was good.

I did not miss being hip,
A gypsy off on a trip.
I put on a suit
And felt absolute-
Ly fine with a brown leather grip.
Style is b.s. Just live
And muster the gifts you can give.
Some very profound
Radicals walk around
Looking trim and conservative.

I drove to work at 4 a.m. past dark houses, a kitchen light burning here and there, got to the studio and switched on the transmitter. I felt like a shepherd tending his flock. My troubles evaporated when I got the morning radio show. The sorrowful birch boughs calling like ghosts disappeared and the dark boat and the owl with the broken wing. At 6 a.m. people have their own griefs and don't need to hear about mine. I turned myself from a pseudo-embittered semi-intellectual into a cheerful avuncular morning radio host of the sort I'd grown up listening to. The Midwestern way. There is nothing special about your loneliness, everyone else has their own, so lighten up.

> Sadness is just like carbuncles:
> Yours is the same as your uncle's
> Whereas the hilarious
> Is wildly various
> Like the wildlife found in the jungles.

Radio was like lawn mowing, which my mother recommended to me when I was a whiny child. *Go out and make yourself useful and you'll feel better.* And she was right. I was a lucky duck, paid a living wage to be cheerful and smart on the air. I played Bach and the Beach Boys, Renaissance dances and doo-wop, and created sponsors like Powdermilk Biscuits, Jack's Auto Repair, and Bebopareebop Rhubarb Pie.

> Invented a hometown up there
> And a sponsor, Jack's Auto Repair,
> And the tasty and mystic
> Powdermilk Biscuit
> For the courage to stay on the air.

> No comedian nor a musician,
> Performance was not my ambition,
> But I was drawn on
> By Lake Wobegon
> And by broadcasting tradition:

> Fibber McGee, Bob and Ray,
> Charlie Weaver, Nichols and May,
> The Grand Ole Opry,
> Roy Rogers, Gene Autry,
> All the ones I had loved yesterday.

Gone was the haughty little poseur of *The Ivory Tower*, liberated to become the amiable breakfast pal, cheerfully tolling off the weather forecast, followed by a medieval tootfest and Thelonious Monk and a monastic *Sanctus*. And then someone calls in from Prescott and wants to hear the "Meditation" from *Thaïs* and instead I give them:

> What can one say of Prescott?
> A happening place it is not.
> Some stores, a gas station,
> And as destination
> It's sort of a burial plot.

I told jokes, of course. A woman called in and asked me to wish her dad a happy birthday. She said, "He's Unitarian and he loves Unitarian jokes." I could think of only one—only time you hear Jesus Christ mentioned in a Unitarian church is when the janitor slips on the stairs—and listeners called in with more. Old Unitarians try to die on the second Thursday of the month, when the recycling is picked up. No interest in heaven because Unitarians aren't in favor of gated communities and in heaven there is perfect harmony, no disagreement, which is torture to Unitarians. Unitarian Ku Klux Klanners go around at night burning question marks in people's yards. I even made my own contribution:

> There was an old Unitarian,
> A ferocious Christmas contrarian.
> "God was not made flesh,"
> He said, so his crèche
> Was a room with just Joseph and Mary in.

> An old atheist of Wilkes-Barre
> Left the Lutheran lunch in a hurry.
> At the feast of Lucia
> There was bad diarrhea.
> He had soaked the herring in curry.

I was upbeat. I read aloud from the police reports in the Northfield news-paper, all about barking dogs and loud music, scattered trash, marital arguments, missing cats. I played requests. People called in and asked me to wish someone a happy birthday and sometimes I played them a song, sometimes wrote a verse.

A big happy birthday to Tiffany
And the gift of daily epiphany:
May she discover
(She and her lover)
Perpetual pleasant polyphony.

There was a young woman named Steph,
Who said, "Some people are deaf.
It's perfectly clear
But they cannot hear
That my name is not spelled with an F."

My listeners took particular pleasure in limericks about public radio.

There was an old man so embittered
At how he had wasted and frittered
His best years away
By listening all day
To reruns of *All Things Considered*.

There was a young girl at Bryn Mawr
Who only tuned in NPR,
And so she believed
That kids are conceived
At a Planned Parenthood seminar.

Here's to the great Ira Glass
Who tends to mumble, alas.
I can't tell from his voice

If he's reading James Joyce,
Speaking Swedish, or saying High Mass.

The humorist David Sedaris
Writes books with titles like *There Is*
A Fish in the Toilet
And *Boredom: Why Spoil It?*
And *A Pair Is* Le Couple *In Paris.*

I have to make an admission:
I never hear *Morning Edition*
Except during Lent
At the convent
Where it's meant as an act of contrition.

For a lawyer in Moorhead, I composed a double:

Hail to the counselor John
Who argued whereof and thereon
With foes and allies,
Then looked in her eyes
And united himself with LaVonne.
Now as you turn 54
Looking out at the Red River shore,
May you continue
To express what's in you
But remember that Less may be More.

He was charmed, of course. He'd been honored and certified but never limericized.

Happy birthday, Jane in Duluth,
Who avoids the crude and uncouth.
She tried to swear once
And felt guilty for months
And that was way back in her youth.

Happy birthday to Maryanne Flint.
They thought she did but she dint.
But Lord if she had
She'd have driven us mad
In ways the newspaper can't print.

Writing limericks was a pleasure and a revelation. It took me back to where I started out as a kid, in Mrs. Shaver's classroom, sunshine pouring in the big windows, me bent over the tablet, No. 2 pencil in hand, writing words for the sensual pleasure of it, fat vowels, the elegant tails of the P and J and Q. A pleasure one step up from making roadways and fortresses in a sandpile. No connection to ego and the desperate quest for approval and acclaim.

I came to KSJR from the University of Minnesota radio station where management was wary of trouble or oddity or drama of any sort, knowing that academic bureaucracy is carnivorous and feasts on trouble and, given an opening, deans and chairmen and vice presidents could chew on it for years, but KSJR had no bureaucracy, only the bare bones of staff, and my boss Mr. Kling was young and ambitious and looking to make a mark.

The radio man William Kling
Carefully set out to bring
A station auspicious,
Where the ambitious
Could create just about anything,
Jazz, interviews,
Or a show where the news
Was imbued with a fictional ring.

My future in radio was given a big bump upward when a young woman named Mary D. Kierstead, whose job it was to comb through the slush pile of unsolicited manuscripts at *The New Yorker*, pulled out some stories of mine and sent them upstairs and I got published there. For a Midwesterner, publication in the magazine was like a knighthood, except better. I went from *announcer* to *auteur*. Word got around. Eventually I wrote a novel, and then another and another, and the love of *scribblescribble* served me well. I could do it for hours and when blocked here, would jump over there and keep scribbling ahead. Other writers found it painful to get stuck but the truth was—they were singles hitters swinging for the fences. Writing was hard for them, but so would golf be, or raising tomatoes. They were perfectionists committed to the nobility of defeat. Me, I write for amusement, and for the pleasure of being paid to have a good time, and all I need is coffee.

> Give me coffee lest I go slack
> And spend the day in the sack
> And never get up
> So bring me a cup,
> Caffeinated—no cream, thank you—black.

I became a Public Service Limerick Provider. People wrote in to request one and if I didn't have time, I sent a generic (*Here's Happy Birthday to you./We admire all that you do./You are worthy of praise/On a hundred birthdays/And here you are just twenty-two.*) and if inspired, I wrote a personal one, such as this for an English teacher in North Dakota turning seventy after having gotten out from under some worrisome health symptoms.

> This poem is in honor of Jim
> On the occasion of him
> Turning three score and ten
> On earth among men
> And not among bright seraphim.
>
> He was born in the town of Northwood
> And brought up to do as he should,
> To be kind (but pragmatic)
> And vote Democratic
> And speak up and be understood.

A loyal prairie progressive
Suspicious of pomp and excessive
Wealth and such
And making too much
Out of what there ought to be less of.

His entire life has been graced
By common sense and good taste
And two rules in mind:
Always be kind
And avoid (if possible) waste.

We beseech the God we adore
His spirits to daily restore
And in the event he
Survives turning seventy
To grant him seventy more.

As a serious poet, I'd been devoted to dramatizing my own dark moods, trying to manufacture despair out of mild distress, and it was liberating to put my literacy at the service of others, strangers who in the dark before a winter dawn needed some support, however slight.

A capable woman named Janet
Seems quite at home on this planet
And the tides and seasons
Occur for good reasons
As if it were Janet who ran it.

The wife of a sixth-grade teacher asked for one for him, saying he was going crazy with three weeks left of the school year:

A sixth-grade teacher named Seth
Sometimes says under his breath
When irked by the tots
Various thoughts

One associates with Lady Macbeth.
He came home and asked for a treaty.
He pleaded: "Be nice to me, sweetie.
I'm feeling wobbly
So pour me a Chablis
And don't be emotionally needy."

He taught in a progressive school, and a poem with homicidal overtones made him laugh out loud, his wife said.

I sat in the studio, playing Beach Boys and Bach and Big Bill Broonzy, taking phone calls from listeners who wanted limericks written, looking at my reflection in the studio window, a thirty-year-old in T-shirt and jeans, mustache, longish hair, who once had been the writer of seriously incomprehensible sociopathic poetry, and now I was scribbling:

O you fabulous babe, Connie Spartz,
Let passion and joy fill our hearts.
Let's have a thrill,
Not sit here in Will-
Mar with all these boring old farts.

And also:

A misanthrope up north in Hawley
Believed human friendship was folly
But he was drawn
To a trumpeter swan
And grew very fond of a collie.

Hawley is up near Moorhead and the limerick drew some mail from people wondering who the misanthrope might be and suggesting a possibility, but he had a cocker spaniel, not a collie. Word got around and our Hawley listenership tripled or quadrupled, from three to twelve. But it wasn't about anybody, it was only for the rhyme. As was this one:

An old fellow from New York Mills
Liked to get tanked to the gills

And drive at midnight

Without a headlight

And a blindfold on just for the thrills.

But there was a real Jan Hatch and I wrote this at the request of a friend of hers.

I'm in love with you, darling Jan Hatch,

I'm the tinder and you are the match.

O Queen of Grand Rapids,

You're the gas, I'm the tappets,

I'm knocking so open the latch.

I was commissioned (gratis) to write a limerick for the fiftieth birthday of Victor Soland, a computer systems analyst known as a nonstop talker. He worked all day with numbers and came home bursting with monologues. I wrote:

A talkative fellow named Soland

Spoke as he drove across Poland,

And continued to talk

All the way to Iraq,

And across the Indian Lowland.

In Bombay, his wife cried out, "Victor!

Do you want to be strangled or kicked, or

Will you be silent?"

In the Indian highland,

He was choked by a boa constrictor.

I was likewise commissioned (no fee) to celebrate the silver wedding anniversary of my high school history teacher Charlie Faust whom I'd kept in touch with, as one should with a person who believes in you against the available evidence.

There was an old scholar named Faust

Who seldom growled or groused

And whose good humor

Was due to the numer-
Ous years he'd been happily spoused

To a woman of legend named Helen,
His Madonna, muse, and Magellan.
Here's to fifty fine years.
Here's to the old dears
Who stayed in what they both fell in.

Some listeners called in requests for limericks for their dog and I had to draw a line: no pet birthdays. None.

I don't own a dog. They're a mess
Of misery and mournfulness
And you never know why
And then one day they die
And you weep. It's embarrassing. Yes.

A woman called and asked for one for her dad who was dying and still telling jokes:

For Bernie up in Baudette,
Where stories are bawdy, you bet,
And men smoking smokes
Tell dirty jokes
Till everyone's trousers are wet.

A simple transaction: she was pleased, and the audience was bemused at the bold irreverence. It's a good limerick. There's no such thing as a great limerick, just as there are no great apple pies or tuna casseroles. Goodness is good enough. If you aim for greatness, you're likely to get fatuity instead.

This is also a good limerick, which I wrote for myself. You could say the same thing in 4,000 words but this is more memorable.

We live by humor and grace,
Good manners, books, an embrace,

Good water, good light,

A pencil to write,

And a bright orange stub to erase.

So, on public radio, the medium of Unitarians, reference librarians, bird-watchers, Henry James readers, and women with more than four cats, I found a happy home. I earned a living talking about Lutheran dairy farmers and the big Fourth of July celebration with the Living Flag and the wonder of Christmas and then the long trial of winter, during which I wrote cautionary verse warning against the urge to go South. It was what my audience wanted to hear on those bitter cold mornings in January when they had to start up their frozen Chevy and drive to school and face a roomful of silent stone-faced sophomores and coax them to take a passing interest in the election of 1912 and the defeat of the Bull Moose progressives of Theodore Roosevelt. They dread those dull eyes and slack faces. They deserve a little pre-school amusement. And so I was inspired to write my first limerick epic. It wasn't for me, it was for them.

There was an old man who was not

Fond of cold winters and got

Away to Santa Fe

And one sunny day

Had a heatstroke and died on the spot.

The widow decamped for Key West

And lay in the sunshine undressed

And was broiled and fried,

Got cancer and died,

Was cremated, then laid to rest.

Her oldest boy tried a high-rise

In Miami where to his surprise

A white albatross

High on hot sauce

Dove down and pecked out his eyes.

His sister in Key Biscayne
Recovered from sorrow and pain
Through gentle massage
Which released a barrage
Of blood clots into her brain.

Her husband, John, cried, "Aha!"
And bought a place in Panama
Where a poisonous snake
Jumped out of a cake
And bit him and also his ma.

His nephew went to Cancún
And joined a Moonie commune
And cashed in his chips
When a lunar eclipse
Made him swoon and choke on a prune.

His brother tried to persist, he
Headed for Corpus Christi
But the weather was misty,
The highway was twisty
And covered with slime,
And it doesn't rhyme
But he slammed into a bridge abutment.

One daughter, observing this all,
Moved back to live in St. Paul.
She's now eighty-three,
Lives happily
Near me and goes nowhere at all.

The quest for comfort and ease
Led to severe tragedies.

They crashed and burned
And nobody learned:
Man should not curse it, he
Thrives on adversity.
God send us more suffering, please.

4

Innovation

THE STANDARD LIMERICK is good enough and one never tires of working within the classic lines. Nobody is out to extend the tennis court or the bowling alley or shorten the free-throw line from fifteen feet. And the limerick of three three-anapest lines wrapped around two double anapests is where a writer matches himself against the greats.

> When the angel of death shall transport
> Me to face God's supreme holy court,
> The Lord will soon note
> All the verses I wrote,
> Of five lines, three long and two short.

My slight contribution to limericism was to add an interior rhyme in the last line to echo the dings of the third and fourth lines, e.g.:

> A young Baptist lady of Aspen
> Fell down groanin' and gaspin'.
> She thought she'd been bit
> By a snake on her tit
> But it was her Sunday school class pin.

This started out with the word "Aspen," which "Baptist" jangled with in an interesting way, then the only rhyme I could come up with, "gaspin'," the triple interior (*bit, tit, it*), and then pure inspiration: the lady was bitten by her own righteousness.

> A young woman came from St. Peter
>
> To St. Paul to get into theater.
>
> And she got her start
>
> By playing a part
>
> In a downtown Walmart as a greeter.

It's a nifty twist—*start, part, mart*—and it adds a degree of difficulty. And then there is this:

> An Episcopalian in Billings
>
> Hears messages through his fillings
>
> That seem to be sent
>
> By a woman in Kent
>
> Who would do thrilling things for ten shillings.

And this, for rhyming felicity multiplicity:

> A liberal lady of D.C.
>
> By day was tasteful and p.c.
>
> And then after ten
>
> She went out with men
>
> Who were rednecks, vulgar and greasy.
>
> "When it comes to the masculine specie,"
>
> She said, "believe me, I'm easy,
>
> But liberals guys
>
> Tend to theologize
>
> And I's ain't St. Clare of Assisi."

It's like adding a half gainer to a forward triple-somersault dive and it lends a delicate echoing chord to the thing:

A young man drank Leinenkugel.

It was cheap and he had to be frugal.

Then he found videos

Of girls with no clothes

Drinking beer from a hose, thanks to Google.

The Internal Third Rhyme is especially effective for a subject with two good rhyming names such as the editor Liz Van Hoose:

I'm fond of my editor Liz,

A whiz in the publishing biz,

Who is easy and loose

But can give it a goose

When it's useful, which often it is.

It's good for the beginner to follow the form scrupulously—*A demented fellow named Garrison couldn't tell Spaniard from Saracen, could not find his pants and didn't know France is the nation that you will find Paris in.*—but eventually love of the limerick leads one to loosen up the bindings and innovate. Once I came up with a perfect six-line limerick:

Rainfall is good for the corn,

Which was true before you were born.

It washes your car,

Fills the town reservoir,

And if it makes you forlorn,

Well, blessed are they who mourn.

And this, loose as it is, is true to the spirit of the limerick though not the form:

A Nashville guy, Dennis Hennesy,

Misspelled "penis" as *pennis*. He

Had gone to college, he

Studied biology,

And had dated women in Tennessee

And somehow missed this knowledge. He
Had physiology
Diagrams—what did Dennis see
To put that extra n
Into the gen-
Italia of men?

That is a triple-diverted augmented expressionist limerick. No rules, you just follow the rhymes.

I came to think of the five-liner as a basic house to which one could add a porch. Or an extra room.

A saintly manager, Gail,
Has a simple technique that can't fail:
At home or at work,
When things go berserk,
Faced with extortion, blackmail,
The angry cries
Of former allies,
Uprisings on a large scale,
She will stop, close her eyes, and inhale.

The hyperlimerick, or extended limerick, is a welcome break from the customary, like if Dorothea Lange had taken a weekend away from her Dust Bowl families and shot color photos of Beverly Hills, like if John Cage had set electronic music aside and written "When My Sweetie Synthesizes Me," if Edward Hopper had painted Fourth of July parades instead of those bleak sunlit houses.

A Lutheran lady in Reno
Stayed up all night playing keno
On the strength of some pills
And the sight of large bills
And a handsome young dealer named Gino.
She was taken with him,

His fingers so slim,
He was graceful and suave and Latino,
And she felt not so bad
As she lost all she had,
Including her cherry (maraschino).

"How long does it take to write a limerick like that?" people ask. The answer is: it comes quickly or it doesn't come at all. You don't sit around waiting for it. Nobody struggles to finish a limerick. There is no such thing as limerick block. People are not driven to drink by the failure to find a tricky rhyme. You simply forget about it or you do it. I tend to do it.

Adam's the obvious perp, he's
The goon, the bum, and the twerp, he's
Caused all the grief
By lifting Eve's leaf
And left her with a bad case of herpes.

I was glad to leave behind the elegy and dirge and lament. There are a hundred things available daily that will bring us to tears; we need art for amusement.

Farewell to poets of sorrow
Wheeling their narrow wheelbarrow
Full of regrets,
Lost love and bad bets,
The Straight Arrow Sad Hero Bureau.

Poets, escape from the pharaoh.
God has his eye on the sparrow.
Head for Sonora
First thing tomorra
Wipe your tracks clean. Be thorough.

New territory, *mio caro.*
A man in a flowered sombrero

Who runs the café
Will hire you today
And he has a daughter, named Charo.

Love in your heart and bone marrow,
Unfurrow your brow, caballero.
Make your heart full.
Tomorrow, the bull,
Tonight the ballet and bolero.

I always take paper and pen to a Twins game so that during those long middle innings I am not at a loss for amusement. People who think baseball is boring are people who are unable to call on their inner resources. I go to a game with friends so there's conversation: a new pitcher comes in from the bullpen to warm up and I turn to my sister and say, "So what was the idea behind the Numerical Bible?" and we discuss that for a minute until play resumes. Or I can write a limerick.

Baseball's a slow game, no doubt.
And a fan can go strolling about
For a bratwurst with mustard
And a soft frozen custard,
And why not a bottle of stout?
Come back to your place,
Still no one on base,
Same score and nobody out.
You sit with your thoughts
Then notice your brat's
Incomplete and you go back for kraut.
And thoughtfully
You go off to pee
When the crowd gives out a great shout
And you wash your hands
And run back to the stands

Expecting you missed a great clout
But it's a young hound
On the field, chased around
By an usher, an ump, and a Scout.

I wrote one for an old pal who used to be the Queen of the Autoharp on my radio show and then, having taken the instrument as far as it could go, she turned to the heroic work of bringing perfection to the world.

My editor Stephanie Beck,
Spectacles hung round her neck,
Slowly goes through
With a sharp No. 2
To review and check and re-check.
She crosses out "that" and writes "which,"
Changes "corner" to "niche."
Like a marshal on TV,
The tireless Stevie
Is the law, and I love her, the bitch.

I know she will laugh at the last line and then she will probably remove the hyphen from "re-check."

❧ 5 ❧

The Limerick Life

I CARRY PENS in my pocket, as you can see from the ink stains, and I carry 5-by-7 sheets of paper folded in half. I write limericks on them to fill up the empty spaces of life that get larger and larger as I get older. Some people fill time by listening to the radio; I don't because I was on radio for years and heard it all. So I pull out a pen and write.

> We are waiting here for a bus
> And I don't want to create a fuss
> But there is a terrorist—
> Look over there—her wrist-
> Watch is a bomb meant for us.

Some of my best work was done in waiting rooms at the Mayo Clinic in Rochester, Minnesota, which rescued me from decrepitude on several occasions. I sat patiently, trying not to brood about what might possibly await. I went for the ritual checkup and was given a little plastic cup and directed toward the men's room where I used the antiseptic pad to clean the *glans* and I stood in the stall waiting for urine to flow and thought of the word *urine* and words that rhyme with it.

> I'm trying to bring forth some urine
> At a medical clinic, secure in

Knowing I've peed
Whenever I need-
Ed, so help me Martin Van Buren.
Just pee in the cup
About halfway up
For a lab technician to stir in
Some little dye
To indicate I
Have cancer for which there's no cure. In
Silence I stand,
Gadget in hand,
And think of my true love and her in
The room where they wait.
I urinate,
The test's negative,
So I shall live
And take her to Naples and Turin.
Off we shall go
And she'll never know
The tragedy we almost were in.

A few hours later, with my eyes dilated, I waited for my ophthalmologist, Dr. Khanna, to perform a cataract/glaucoma procedure to allow me to go on reading and writing for a while longer. She is a professional who offers the same excellent care to each and every one and yet I want her to know that I'm a writer, so I handed her a limerick. A reminder that my eyes are my livelihood.

My eye surgeon, good Dr. Khanna,
Looked through her eyepiece down on a
Novelist's retina
Who thought he was gettin' a
Vision of the blessed Madonna.

I recited it to her and she laughed without losing her focus on the new lens she was placing in my right eye. And then for her nurse Julie, who held my head while a suture was removed:

> An ophthalmic nurse name of Julie
> Holds my head steadily, coolly,
> As I undergo
> A procedure that's so
> Irritating I may get unruly.

I said, "Julie, if you ever have a painful eye procedure, I want to be the one who holds your head," and she said, "Take a number and get in line."

Everything worked out well though recovery was slow and I wondered what I'd do with my life if clarity didn't return.

> What will I do if I'm blind
> To keep from losing my mind?
> I'll be very obnoxious
> And rob the poorboxes
> And send threatening letters unsigned.

> And instead of a smart German shepherd,
> I will have on a leash a big leopard
> Who will snarl as I
> Make sure each passerby
> With violent curses is peppered.

> A writer depends on his eyes
> And when malfunctions arise,
> Taste, hearing, and touch
> Don't matter that much,
> Though sex is a lovely surprise.

> So here I am, sweetheart of mine,
> Hoping that you'll cross the line

And I'll pledge allegiance
To your lower regions.
I'm here. In the dark. My sunshine.

I go to St. Mary's Hospital in Rochester for the implantation of a pacemaker. In school, I looked down on nerdy kids who did well in math and chemistry, and now my life depends on them. My heart sometimes hesitates 3.8 seconds between beats. At 5, you faint and fall down and bang your head. So I lie on a gurney and am wheeled into Surgical Prep. I have brought paper and pen, and my nurse Kim says, "You're going to be sedated, you know."

"When?"

"As of five minutes ago."

Well, a man needs a challenge. So I write her a limerick.

A cardiac nurse name of Kim
Says, "The chances of failure are slim.
You're not going to die."
And she points to the sky.
"Any questions? Address them to Him."

No patient ever wrote her a limerick before. She is impressed and wheels me into the OR. It's a beautiful sedative. I'm still cognizant of people around, voices, the clink and beep and hum of hardware, and I appreciate the coordination of the team, and the anesthetist who keeps me informed of what she's putting into me, as if I actually understood.

Meredith who did anesthesia
Said, "It won't lead to amnesia
But this sedation
May cause constipation.
We recommend milk of magnesia."

I wrote this as Dr. Bradley was scoping out the incision site. A very nice man whose parents were doctors, a neurologist and a pathologist. He grew

48

up in southeast Minneapolis. He was a little kid running around on the playground when I was a grad student at the U. I asked what type of pacemaker he'd be installing and he was glad to discuss the merits of Medtronic vs. Boston Scientific vs. another one, I forget the name. So I wrote a few lines for him.

> The electrophysiologist Bradley
> Said, "This pacemaker I admit sadly
> Won't increase IQ
> But what it will do
> Is prevent your heart beating madly."

The device is the size of a wristwatch, minus the band, and a wire extends from it down into the base of your heart where it's anchored by a screw that your heart creates scar tissue around, and there it sits, stimulating a steady 60 beats per minute for the next ten years until the battery needs to be replaced.

The pacemaker did not improve brain function, I found in the airport, heading for New York, when I pulled out my billfold and saw no driver's license. Check pockets, briefcase. Credit cards, no license. The brain flutters. Taxi? Pickpocket? Dementia? Loss of license today, tomorrow I can't conjugate "lay" and "say," next day my wife's name is missing along with the three branches of government. Then my license is found. In jacket pocket. I head for TSA, resuming my life as a certified person. Life is precarious. So much depends on a small card with a grim picture of me on it. Lose it and I become a fugitive, stateless, displaced. I board the plane to New York and squeeze into my seat and I do what I need to do to dispel the fear of dementia. I write.

> I'm seated in 17C
> And 16 leans back on me.
> I could cut his throat
> But he'd bleed on my coat
> And stain it permanently.

Minnesotans, to anger, are slow.
We're descended from martyrs, you know.
But my crippled knee
Can be made comedy
And a limerick is what makes it so.

In the limerick he lets out a fart
That rips his trousers apart
Along the seam
And his self-esteem
Is shattered and it breaks his heart.

His career goes right down the chute:
Deserted, diseased, destitute,
He lives in a hut,
A kick in the butt,
All because he let out a poot.

I have two hours and I launch into a New York series. All around me men
are reading newspapers, women reading novels, millennials watching TV,
all of which I used to do and don't anymore. The septuagenarian has a
strong sense of Having Seen It All Before and even the daily dishonesty
and corruption of the Trump administration seems like very old news,
whereas "Newark" is a real challenge.

There was a young lady of Newark
Who rode a train daily to work.
Her old job sucked; her
Dream job, conductor,
Opened up, so now she rides through work.

There was a young man of Park Slope
Who liked to be tied up with rope
And forced on his knees

To eat black-eyed peas
But only by friends, one would hope.

There was a young lady of Queens
Fell in love with old college deans
Of science and law
Whose writings she saw
In high-quality magazines.

A man of the Upper West Side
Never left, he was so satisfied,
Till at age fifty-five
He went for a drive
To Vermont, caught brain cancer, and died.

There was a young man of the Bronx
Who was tired of beeps, toots, and honx,
So he went to Surrey
Where they're not in a hurry
And do not say Thanks, they say Thonx.

A priest who served Murray Hill
Said, "If it be the Lord's Will
That I abstain,
Refuse and refrain,
I'll lie in bed perfectly still."

The writing of limericks is a fine use of my time. I go to an arts luncheon at a hotel in Midtown, and a famous soprano stops at our table to say hello. She chats about this and that, she is gracious, but what is on everyone's mind, which nobody can comment on, is the stuff of a limerick.

She bent and her décolletage
Appeared as a golden mirage,
Two pears on a tray,

> Two bowls of white clay,
> Two VWs in the garage.

Rude? Maybe, but how can you ignore them? *There they are.* Bazooms. The limerick gets to the point.

I go up to the St. Luke's ER on West 114th with a painful right ankle and sit in a waiting room with a cast of unfortunates and am attended to by a young physician who is smart and professional and tells me it's not a blood clot, not a fracture, and in the four hours in the waiting room, I write numerous limericks, including one for her:

> The ER doc Elise Levine
> Is dealing with chaos just fine;
> Your calm expertise
> And kindness, Elise,
> Bring the Upper West Side some sunshine
> In the shadow of St. John Divine.

And of course one for my wife, worrying a mile away.

> I'm here in the St. Luke's ER
> And wishing it were a dim bar,
> Three sheets to the wind
> I've met Jenny Lind,
> And thinking, How soon? And How far?

One night we go to Carnegie Hall for the Royal Concertgebouw Orchestra and the Mozart 40th, which is lovely, but what does a man do with the long intermission? I don't feel like standing in a long line to pay twenty bucks for a coffee and a chocolate brownie, and I'm having little memory issues—many people seem to know me whom I ought to know and do not, and it's awkward to feign familiarity without using a name, so I stay in my seat and pull out a pen.

> A mellow young man who played cello,
> A very inventive young fellow,

Suddenly found
He got a great sound
When he filled it with bright yellow Jell-O.

So then he took up the viola
And filled it half full of granola
And some folks applauded
And cheered but good God it
Was shit with a dash of Shinola.

So then he tried violin
And violets were what he put in
Until TSA
Took away the bouquet
Before violence could begin.

And finally he picked up the bass
And there found passion and grace.
Young women go
For a man who gets low:
I'll show you. Stand still in your place.

My wife returns after intermission, and there is an ad in the program for Bank of America with plenty of white space. The Brahms's Fourth is the second half and I can feel her absorption in it. Probably she played it back in her student days and now, even without violin in hand, she feels focused on it. I feel focused on her. The arm next to mine.

I really don't want to obsess
But you bring me pure happiness!
Magnificent you,
Your light shining through,
As you step out of your dress.

She reads it and puts her hand on my knee. This makes Brahms more meaningful to me. I'm a romantic. I wrote a book of sonnets back in my sixties, sonnets about mortality and the power of love to overcome shame and regret, and was pleased with it, and the book disappeared like a pebble dropped into the Arctic Ocean, nobody said one word about it. I saw a copy years later at a yard sale among the humorous plaques and novelty socks, the shirt that said, "Help Me, I've Fallen And I Cannot Reach My Beer," the unused exercise bike, the unread books, including my sonnets, mint condition, 35 cents. I bought it, of course. A poet doesn't want a good book to go so cheaply. Some writers create a brand of mournful reverie and deliver a truckload of it annually and are well-regarded and others, like me, feel inspired to abandon our competency for something that amuses us. I've disappointed plenty of loyal readers who came to the diner for eggs and hash browns and coffee and found watermelon meringue and hibiscus tea. People were often disappointed by the News from Lake Wobegon when it wandered away from the town and into the woods of the personal essay. But I am the boss and I can do as I please, which won't always be so. Someday I won't have so many marbles and so I need to be adventurous while it's possible. The impulse to write sonnets came about when I memorized four of Shakespeare's for a Poetry Month speech at a high school. The kids were impressed. I was even more impressed by the perfection of them in my mouth, and so I waded into the sonnet. I wrote a hundred of them. Now I'm caught up with the limerick, which I loved as a kid. Imagine a sculptor in his dotage sitting on a beach, creating rectangular forms out of wet sand.

> The limerick is quite evanescent
> And lives in a very brief present
> But if I produce
> One that's vulgar and loose,
> It may well be incandescent.

The next day, I ride the downtown B train to 42nd Street and Sixth Avenue, which is close to the old offices of *The New Yorker* and also Town Hall where I used to do a radio show, back when I was a big shot. The magazine quit the field of light verse long ago, abandoned the screwball for the Inscrutable, but I wrote a few rhyming verses and submitted them and the poetry editor handed them back and smiled and shook her head.

> The editor dear Alice Quinn
> Likes poems about grief and chagrin,
> Not laughing hyenas,
> Nebraska, your penis,
> Or personal redemption from sin.

I once wrote a limerick for the editor William Shawn when we had lunch at the Algonquin on 44th. A slice of dry toast and a pot of hot water for him, a cheeseburger and fries for me. I was in awe of him and couldn't bring myself to say what I wanted to say, which was "Could I resume A. J. Liebling's 'The Wayward Press' column?" So we sat and talked about Liebling. I didn't send him the limerick I wrote:

> The great editor William Shawn
> Sang the blues one night before dawn,
> Inserting a comma
> After "Yo mama,"
> And before "she gone she am gone."

Walking up West 44th I felt I was in a time warp and that my hero A. J. Liebling was alive and might come striding down the street, wire-rimmed glasses and great paunch, and I might see Eudora Welty, as I did years ago, standing in front of the Algonquin Hotel, looking for a taxi, and I'd be 25 again, a pack of Luckies in my pocket, so I walked over to Grand Central into the Oyster Bar, the restaurant that time has not changed. I sat down and the waitress came by, said hello, handed me a menu. She didn't ask how I was doing today—she was a classic New York waitress, a big healthy woman, all business. Came back a few minutes later, said, "Ready?" I ordered black coffee and a half dozen Kumamotos and the grilled halibut. She did not say, "Oh, that's one of my favorites" as millennial waiters in the Midwest do. She brought the coffee and I amused myself by writing a limerick:

> She brought me six Kumamotos
> That were good as in gourmet mag photos
> And salty and creamy
> And made me feel dreamy
> As Ulysses in the land of the lotos.

After she brought the food, she did not come back to say, "How's every-thing tasting?" No need—it's the Oyster Bar, the food is good. Nor did she come back later to ask, "You still working on that?" She was a mini-malist. Waiting on tables is a service; it isn't the beginning of a beautiful friendship.

It dawned on me that I could always come back to the Oyster Bar and be in the America I remember from my youth—the Oyster Bar, Grand Central, and the Public Library. So I walked up Fifth Avenue and climbed the stairs past the great stone lions Patience and Fortitude into the Library and went up to the third floor and the magnificent Rose Reading Room and camped at a long table among young people hard at work on, no doubt, important things and I had nothing to do but amuse myself. We sit in cathedral splen-dor, under a 52-foot ceiling with murals of blue skies and billowy clouds, and we observe a strict decorum conducive to serious work—I imagine that the woman across the table from me is writing a feminist reinterpretation of the American Civil War and now she is looking at me writing on my yellow legal pad.

> I sit in the Rose Reading Room
> Like a weaver addressing his loom
> And with paper and pen
> Work once again
> On limericks like engines. *Vroom.*
> Surrounded by others,
> My sisters and brothers,

Students and readers for whom
Life means learning,
Pages turning,
Enlightenment to consume.
That guy who's obese is
Writing his thesis
On the principles of David Hume
And the girl in green plaid
Is reading Conrad
And her boyfriend (perhaps her bridegroom)
Sitting in bliss, he's
Reading *Ulysses*
And thinking of Leopold Bloom,
While I write verse
About those who disburse
Loud and gaseous fumes,
Gases released
Smelling like the deceased
Somebody tried to exhume.
While my neighbors
Engage in labors,
Illustrious ones, I presume,
For whom cannon should shoot
A massive salute,
Ka-boom, ka-boom, ka-boom.

6

Reverence

I'M A CHRISTIAN so of course I write limericks about others of my ilk. They're the people I know. I wrote one about a Jew just to prove I could, but one was enough.

> An Orthodox rabbi of France,
> One night, strictly by chance,
> Ate escargot
> And saw it was so
> And shuddered and shit in his pants.

> It came from a Gentile grocer
> And was strictly filth and nonkosher.
> The rabbi got drunk
> And when asked by his unc-
> Le, "You okay?" The rabbi said, "No, shir."

Okay. Not great but okay. Not nearly as good as my Baptist ones.

> A Baptist boy in St. James
> Put his parents in silver frames,
> Looking down from the wall,

And if he swore at all,
Their faces burst into flames.

A Baptist preacher of Charlotte
Seduced a Hollywood starlet.
He said, "Don't wear red
When we jump into bed
Or I'll have to assume you're a harlot."

An atheist fellow named Dayton
Believed there's no God and no Satan
So he cursed and he sinned,
Got drunk and broke wind,
And the Baptists sat waitin' and waitin'.

A Baptist girl of Louisville
Attends High Mass for the thrill
Of papist excesses
And men in long dresses,
And confesses her longing to kill
Her brother and mother
And maybe one other
And to seduce Fr. Bill.

This, I believe, is more profound, if profundity is what you're looking for.

A Methodist in Illinois
Said, "Scripture has filled me with joy"
And he whooped and he cheered
Which struck us as weird,
Then he took off his clothes, and oh boy.
What is meant to shock
And make people talk,
In the end, may simply annoy.

And this one I wrote just because I liked the words "God guy."

> An Assembly of God guy in Dallas
> Looked on Baptists with malice.
> "If when you go down
> To be baptized, you drown,
> Don't expect an ivory palace."

I grew up evangelical in Minnesota, the state of taciturn, stoical, coop-erative-minded people schooled by blizzards and subzero cold—in other words, Lutherans. We're all Lutherans here, even the atheists—it's a Lu-theran God they don't believe in. We are elaborately modest and avoid expressing personal preference. We do not, as a rule, hug; there are ex-ceptions but not many. We are wary of charm. We accept depression as a sign of good character. Every two years, we meet in convention and offer resolutions denouncing racism, recidivism, sexism, sarcasm, and materi-alism, which pass unanimously, and we feel a blow has been struck and progress made. We are people of firm principle—no Lutheran would ever commit adultery in a car parked in a space marked *Handicapped Only*.

> Minnesota's the land of mosquitoes,
> Flesh-piercing flying torpedoes,
> Which infect the bloodstream
> With low self-esteem
> And puncture our modest libidos.

> The prairie is flat as can be
> So there's nowhere that God cannot see:
> He knows every thought,
> Every whim, every blot,
> And watches continuously.

We avoided worldliness. We lived in the countryside along the Mississippi River, in a house my dad built himself, with a half-acre garden behind it. We were taught to say *please* and *thank you*, and when lunch was served, to take small helpings and chew with your mouth closed. They were good and kind people. They had high standards, namely *Whatsoever ye do, let it be to the glory of God*. And *Only one life, 'twill soon be past. Only what's done for Christ will last.*

I'm grateful for my good parents and family, and I do not regret that they took a dim view of the limerick. Their resistance to it set me up to explode in laughter when I came across the Legman anthology. They were waiting for the Rapture when they expected to be whooshed up into heaven to meet the Lord. I felt that the God who created the otter, the platypus, the giraffe, and the hippopotamus must have a serious interest in the ridiculous. The purpose of the porpoise is to provide pleasure to the populace. And maybe He is also amused by people who are waiting to be whooshed.

> My family was solid as rock,
> No alcohol, no angry talk.
> *Mens sana, corpore sano,*
> In a home with piano,
> And meals were served by the clock.

> Everyone had his/her place.
> Nice clothes, clean hands and face.
> Meat loaf, potatoes,
> Fried green tomatoes,
> After our dad said the grace.

> I grew up with big radios,
> Comedians, amateur shows,
> Fibber McGee
> & Molly and me,
> And (bass voice) "*The Shadow Knows* ..."

> I grew up, you might say, straight-laced,
> Ambitious but cautious and chaste,
> Obeying the Lord,

Remained above board,
Avoided flamboyance and waste.

Blessed are all those who mourn,
Whose lives are tangled and torn,
And so says the Spirit,
If only we hear it:
To laughter and love were we born.

I trust that after I die
I will fly to His side in the sky,
But if it's not so,
I'll never know.
I could worry about it, but why?

Brethren avoided worldly things, awaiting the Second Coming. When the trumpet sounds and the Lord appears in the sky to take you home to Glory, do you want Him to find you chuckling about naked men counting to twenty-one on their fingers and toes and one more appendage? Perhaps not. The best way to escape worldly snares was to marry a good Brethren woman with a Bible in one hand and a baby in the other and find a low-echelon job that doesn't require you to curry the favor of unbelievers and doesn't pay so much that you're tempted by material things. When I was seventeen, I got the perfect Brethren job: a summer job washing dishes in a scullery at the Evangeline Hotel for single women. But every morning and evening, they trooped up to my scullery window with their trays of dirty dishes and bent down to set the trays on the counter, a parade of blouses bowing, some more unbuttoned than others, and I looked up as I took their plates. Some of them said, "Thank you." One cleavage after another.

A parade of young hotel guests
Pass in their blouses and vests
And the slightest sliver

Of skin makes him shiver
As he tries not to look at their chests.

I sometimes think that if I had settled down at the scullery and learned to look at the sink and not the counter, I'd still be living the Brethren life I was brought up to live. I'd be married to a Prudence or Priscilla who'd make sure the kids and I were dressed and shined up by 8 a.m. on Sunday morning so we wouldn't be late to Sunday school. I'd give out a hymn in Morning Meeting, "O Thou in Whose Presence my soul takes delight, on Whom in affliction I call," and I'd stand at the table in the middle of the room and break the loaf open and pass it for Communion. We'd come home to a pot roast and potatoes and go back to the meeting hall for a lecture on Malachi by a preacher (known as a Laboring Brother) and then a coffee hour during which we'd send gospel tracts ("Where will you spend eternity?") to the families of the recently deceased listed in the *Tribune* obituaries.

God gave me a job washing dishes
But I was wildly ambitious
And fueled by hope,
I could climb up the rope
To become notable and auspicious
On life's slippery slope,
But when I smell soap,
I think, "Beware of your wishes."

Now I'm known from here to Assyria,
The object of mild hysteria,
But I stand at a sink
And smell soap and think,
"I miss that old cafeteria."

7

The Sunday Limerick

I LEFT THE Brethren and skipped church for decades, using Sundays as work days, and in my fifties was happy to find my way into the Episcopal church. I married an Episcopalian. Had she been Quaker, I would've quaked; had she been Jewish, hand me the Torah, Laura. I felt odd living in the secular world among nice people who had never experienced the mystery of faith or been roused by Paul's epistles, who had once been an enemy.

> St. Paul was a first-rate apostle,
> Sent to poke and to jostle,
> And admonish the herd
> To live by the Word
> Lest the faith turn into a fossil.

St. Michael's and St. Mark's were a long throw from the Brethren, but the Word of God changeth not and the prayers moved me, particularly the long meditative Prayers of the People with the silent blanks where one can whisper the names of loved ones in need and those who have died and one feels the community of spirits in the room. I give thanks for blessings and I pray for the afflicted, while contemplating the imbalance, me ensconced in a life of ease, people in North Carolina wiped out by floods. After we confess our sins and are forgiven, we mingle like children at recess, shaking hands. I am not, by and large, moved by the homily and I use the fifteen minutes to write in the bulletin.

> I go to the Church of St. Mark's,
> Not Karl who growls and barks
> But the gentle disciple
> Whose words in the Bible
> Can ward away grizzlies and sharks.
> The acoustics in this church are such
> That the man may be preaching in Dutch
> As I sit in our pew,
> Look over at you,
> And thank the Creator so much
> For this bare, lovely thigh
> In the short skirt that I
> Silently, reverently touch.

A love limerick, with religious overtones. The bare thigh is only for the rhyme—my wife wears a full skirt to church—but everything else is true, particularly the gratitude.

A Gothic cathedral, long with a vaulted ceiling and arches, stained glass, high altar, but the human beings in the pews are not out of a Calvin Klein catalog but out of Hogarth, Walker Evans, Gordon Parks, Rubens, my high school annual, and it was good to hear the readings of Old Testament, Epistle, Gospel, with the chanting of a Psalm, and confess our unworthiness together and after we were absolved, to reach around and shake hands, which in this particular church was like a family reunion, lots of aisle-crossing, arms outstretched, big redemptive smiles.

> The tall man sat still in his pew,
> Doing as sinners must do,
> And during Confession
> Felt some progression,
> The end of a grudge, maybe two,

And sang his bass part

On "How Great Thou Art,"

And felt some mercy pass through,

The fading at last

Of griefs of the past,

A slight turn toward something new,

A new day begun

And what must be done

Is waiting for himself to do.

I love St. Mary the Virgin on 46th Street in Manhattan, known as Smoky Mary's for the generosity of the incense pot. Also for the inaudibility of the homily. A man in a clerical robe stands at the high pulpit under a wooden roof and his mouth moves as if he were talking and you can imagine he's reciting "The Wreck of the Hesperus" or reeling off the lunch menus for the week ahead or eulogizing his dog. I sat in Solemn High Mass, my daughter leaning against my shoulder, dozing, and wrote:

At the Church of St. Mary the Virgin,

We are smoked by incense like sturgeon.

God's holy Word

Can hardly be heard

While the organ clamors

Like the jackhammers

In the city that God put the church in.

The hush of sanctity is conducive to writing and after decades of church attendance, there is rarely anything new in the sermon, neither good nor bad, just a trickle of syrup on the burnt pancakes, which inspires one to limericize. It looks innocent, you writing on the back page of the bulletin as if jotting down notes on the sermon. *1. His death satisfies the law. 2. Dispensation of grace. 3. Liberty of believers. 4. Hope.* Whereas, in fact, you are writing—

An angry old Anglican swore
He'd lost his faith so he tore
His Bible to pieces,
Burned pictures of Jesus,
But God loved him still, maybe more.

In the Episcopal church, lay readers do the Old Testament and Epistle passages, the Psalm is chanted, and the priest processes down the aisle, surrounded by candle-bearers and perhaps a deacon with a smoke pot, to read the Gospel passage, after which he kisses the page. This is impressive to an old fundamentalist who grew up in a church where any man, if moved by the Spirit, stood up and read Scripture, a used-car salesman, a postal clerk, whoever. Episcopalians favor the "Love thy neighbor" side of Scripture and the fundamentalists loved the mysteries, prophecy, the Apocalypse.

The book that we call Revelations
Is full of tremendous sensations
Of fear and trembling
And legions assembling
And the devastation of nations.
It was written by John
In a hot marathon,
Who was on some strong medications.

I sit halfway back, among gay couples and black ladies in big straw hats, one of the few men upholding the old habit of a suit, white shirt, and tie. Others come to the Lord as they are, jeans, T-shirt, sneakers, maybe a jacket, but I like to dress up, not that I think the Lord is fooled, but simply because my uncles did and as a kid I looked forward to adulthood and now here I am.

The sermon is muffled and dim.
I hear the word "Capernaum."
The sentences pass

67

Like ducks in the grass.
I wait patiently for the hymn.

Have mercy upon me, O Lord.
I am weak and willful and bored.
I've abandoned Your Ways
But I kneel in Your praise,
Bless my laptop, which is my sword.

I say the prayer of contrition
And see my pernicious condition,
And then in an inst-
Ant am cleansed, at least rinsed,
A sinner but a newer edition.

I sit in a pew I've chosen for its dim acoustics and during the homily, I write in the margin of the bulletin.

The Prodigal Son has returned
And his brother is pissed off and burned
And refuses to laugh
Or eat fatted calf:
It's injustice where he's concerned.

We sons who have wandered astray
Are enjoying our veal flambé.
In God's grace we trust
And pray that the just
Will forgive us our pleasure someday.

The sermons I dread are the ones that start with a joke. This naked attempt to ingratiate is the opposite of what a sermon is for, which is to touch the conscience or to teach or to do both. The people in the pews around me laugh uncomfortably at the feebleness of the joke and I pull out a pen and find an empty place in the program alongside the *Sanctus* and I write:

I sit here and think of Infinity,
And God who made everything in it, He
Created the frame
But is not to blame
For my toxic male masculinity.

I maintained a grudge against organists for years—too much power in the hands of one tyrant seated up in the loft behind the organ, out of range of sticks and stones—but one night, walking in south Minneapolis, I heard the peal of the pipes from behind stone walls, opened the door, stepped into a dark vestibule and the dim sanctuary. The organ was above my head, in the choir loft. Nobody in the pews.

An organist whom I can't see
Is playing immaculately
And the glorious sound
Is rolling around
For him or her, God, and me.

I admire the organist's fettle
Though I'd wish for more wood and less metal
And stifle the trumpet
And oboe, just dump it,
And ease up on the sound pedal.

Bach is a bountiful myriad
Of blessings and in my theory it
Comes from the Lord
Whom Johann adored
And whatever it means, thank you. Period.

Greetings

I DON'T BUY greeting cards because I am a writer and can write better ones of my own. Your friend the beekeeper doesn't give you a jar of boughten honey and your friend the baker doesn't bring you a loaf of Wonder Bread. I wrote a Get Well card to a teenaged boy in the hospital after an appendectomy.

> The appendix is down in your belly,
> And without it a man does quite well. He
> Will be twice as smart,
> And though he will fart,
> They'll be sweet ones, not rancid and smelly.

Condolence cards are hard but I wrote a limerick once for a friend who lost her brother to suicide. I doubt it was much consolation. So much pain, so few words:

> I'm not a priest or a pastor
> And so I never could master
> The consolation
> Of devastation
> Of those who are met with disaster.
> I'm only a simple broadcaster

But I'm thinking of you
Which I offer in lieu
Of daisies, a rose, or an aster.

It's an okay limerick, as good as a limerick of condolence can be, and she was grateful I took the time to do it. And taking time is the important thing, not trying to tell someone what she should feel.

I write a Christmas card every year, which is easy, a piece of cake.

December can be cold and cruel,
And that's why we grab onto Yule.
An excuse for delight,
Bright bulbs in the night,
And also two weeks off from school.

Cookies and carols and candles,
Evergreens strewn on the mantels,
And a tree wound with strings
Of various things,
And that famous chorus of Handel's.

Meanwhile it snows on us all
From the woods to the walk and the wall.
It's Past and it's Present
All made luminescent
In one transcendental snowfall.

It's a village in Russia—Tolstoy—
Hans Brinker, the little Dutch boy,
Jim and Della and Clara,
The Victorian era,
Feliz Navidad.
Spread the tidings abroad.
Thanks be to God.
Silent night—jingle bells—joy.

It's not easy being old. People you know die and usually it's the wrong ones. Your hearing fades and people nearby are talking about transcendental medication and you wonder why you haven't heard about it before. Your wife suggests a restaurant that offers ballet parking and it's disappointing when the attendants don't dance. Birthdays and anniversaries don't matter much when you get old—the numbers are frightening. But I write notes to friends as inspiration strikes. I neglected them during my ambitious middle age, and then the ambitions burnt themselves out and now its friendship that matters. And the diminution of ambition is a great blessing.

The writer Patricia Hampl lives around the corner and we are so respectful of each other's work that we never knock on the other's door. I imagined she'd gone off to New York or Prague; she imagined I was on the road doing shows. But whenever we do meet, it's the same as it was fifty years ago when we were students at the University. She's a loyalist, all the way.

> My sister of letters Pat Hampl
> Writes memoirs that set an example
> That one can live large
> On life's steady march
> And not look for icons to trample.
> Catholic, Democrat, teacher:
> Attention, her primary feature;
> Elegance, wit,
> An ear for bullshit,
> And affection for God's every creature.
> Memory is her material,
> The mundane and the ethereal.
> The gifts the day gives,
> The street where she lives,
> The strawberries on her hot cereal.

I wrote one for Roy Blount whose writing I admired, which led me to drive up to his house in the Berkshires and introduce myself. We threw a football around and drank beer and talked about things. This was long before Facebook, back when you friended people in person.

> The humorist Mr. Roy Blount
> Had gravy stains on his front
> And said with a drawl,
> "Ha y-doin', y'all?"—
> They thought he was drunk, but he wunt.

> A Georgian by birth, Mister Roy
> Combines critic and good ole boy.
> He is up for what's new
> But the Good and the True
> Are qualities time can't destroy.

An Ohioan, Ian Frazier, is the Liebling of today except his landscape is broader and he writes better. His memoir *Family* is a classic and *Great Plains* and *Coyote v. Acme* and books on Siberia and fishing and the Bronx.

> A nonfiction man, Ian Frazier,
> Performs miracles through erasure.
> In his book *Great Plains*,
> He wiped out two lanes
> Of freeway by moving a glacier.
> And a rogue coyote
> Who was crazed on peyote,
> He trimmed with disposable razor.
> Ian, whom I know as Sandy,
> Writes on paper by hand. He
> Writes, in straight lines,
> Prose that combines
> Mark Twain with Tolstoy and Gandhi.

> I'm in love with Emmylou Harris
> With whom I vacationed in Paris
> And walked by the Seine
> As handsome French men
> Envied me for who *ma chère* is.

None of which is true but a man can think what he thinks.

And in 2005, when Meryl Streep won big awards for her evil role in *Prada* and my movie with Robert Altman got nothing, I flashed her a rhyme.

> I'm THRILLED you were honored for *Prada*
> And for my little film—nothing. Nada.
> Don't mind in the least.
> I am an artiste
> And a man's gotta do what he's gotta.

> Out here on the prairie, it's level
> And no place for pride, lust, or revel
> Or extravagant dress
> Or covetousness
> Of awards for playing the Devil.

And she responded forthwith:

> *So* Prada *pranced down the red carpets*
> *While Prairie, so witty, so sharp—its*
> *Meandering story*
> *Defied category*
> *In the Land of the La Brea Tar Pits.*

A movie star who can toss off a first-class limerick is astonishing, but she was astonishing even before she wrote it; she makes a practice of astonishment.

My radio show was managed for forty years by three women, Margaret Moos, Christine Tschida, and Kate Gustafson, and as a result of their dedication, savvy, and pizzazz, and that of the *PHC* staff in general, I was (and I am) completely ignorant of the business of putting on shows, traveling, contracts, finance, broadcast rights, online distribution, and much more, I'm sure. Kate is the long-term boss, from 2001 to present, and I assume she will stick around until she needs to make Last Arrangements. I'd like a traditional Episcopal Mass, no eulogies, lots of old hymns, a brief homily on Redemption, a large well-remunerated choir to sing the Fauré *Requiem,* and coffee and doughnuts afterward, and for Communion, my cousin Susie's bread and a good Portuguese port wine, hang the expense.

> Kate G, the manager/master,
> Has saved my ass from disaster,
> Fatal collisions
> From foolish decisions,
> Treacherous turns
> That later one learns
> Definitely
> Led to a tree,
> Nothing but nothing gets past her.
> Accountant and nurse,
> I write her this verse
> Which she'd recommend
> Should now come to an end.

Late in my career, I hired an assistant, Katharine Seggerman, who responded to an online ad, who turned out to be the in-house critic and editor I'd dreamed of finding for fifty years. She had been unavailable because she hadn't been born until midway in those fifty years.

> Katharine, the best of assistants,
> I'm grateful for her existence:
> Scarily smart,
> Generous of heart,
> Keen, analytic,

Editor, critic,
Good humor combined with persistence.
I'd be a beggarman
Without Ms. Seggerman
To assist me in going the distance.

9

Heroes

I'M A WRITER because I love being indoors, especially since I dread getting Lyme disease, which is transmitted by ticks, a disease that brings on headaches, fatigue, painful joints, diarrhea, nausea, facial paralysis, and makes you feel 87 years old, which will come soon enough without your having to traipse around outdoors. If you need wilderness, Ansel Adams took pictures of it: look at them and spritz yourself with pine cologne. Whatever there is to be learned from living in the woods Thoreau already wrote it. Unfortunately, he admonished the young to dare to march to their own drummer, and now you see them wearing headphones, bobbing their heads to their personal beat, ignoring the people around them because Thoreau said, "U gottta be U. Nuts to the norm. School is out, bro. Go 4 it." But once long ago I went to a literary event where a great outdoorsman walked up to me and started stuttering, the wandering essayist Edward Hoagland, author of an adventurous misfit memoir, *Compass Points*, which I admired so much I was speechless, meeting him. We formed an inarticulate friendship and I wrote him an ode.

> The explorer/essayist Ted
> Hoagland went forging ahead
> To Africa, Juneau,
> Not *pluribus, uno,*

The Arctic, too—or so I read.
A man with a stammer
Like a pneumatic hammer:
"Open the gates!
Great richness awaits!
Go forth to be fêted!" he said.
Meanwhile I lay in my bed,
Hoagland marching ahead.

In his memoirs he confesses
To various sins and excesses
And consorting gaily
At Barnum & Bailey
With lions and lionesses.

I trotted along everywhere,
From Sudan to Washington Square,
Each green leafy address,
Then rose from the mattress
And settled myself in a chair.

It's a good idea for a limerick—a writer so brilliant he makes it unnecessary
for you to follow in his footsteps, the work being complete in itself and
requiring no disciples. And those are my heroes: A. J. Liebling, Flannery
O'Connor, John Updike—who could hope to imitate any of them? I only
ever worshipped writers, no radio announcers because radio is a steam-
roller that makes everyone shallow, some are of a thicker shallowness, but
it's impossible to do with radio what Hoagland does—to take you along
with his boyhood self, a stuttering oddball, escaping from the stratified
social world into the paradise of ponds and woods in the rural Connecticut of his youth. You can read those chapters over and over and they still
come alive for you.

Whenever I did a show in northern Wisconsin, a man named Jerry
came and brought me a pound of wild rice that he had harvested. He was

Chippewa and thought my stories were really about his people. So I wrote five lines on a sheet of paper, signed it with a flourish, and gave it to him.

> There is an old man on the Rez
> Who was here to welcome Cortez
> And he took Captain Cook
> Around for a look
> And Lewis and Clark, so he says.

He laughed. A genuine laugh. He folded it and put it in his pocket.

I went to the White House for a ceremony at which the president spoke and I stood where I could see his teleprompter. It was impressive. He was improvising like crazy and his improv was funnier than the script. I loved the Obamas. So much weight on their shoulders, being the First A-A President and First Lady, but they were the most natural big shots I ever met in my life, warm, cool, funny, and together they made the country proud. Only a very dedicated redneck living deep in the swamp of Fox News could manage to dislike them.

> Our president Barack Obama
> Had a black dad and white mama.
> He is cool, he can bop,
> And yet he will stop
> And participate in Bowlerama.

> And Mrs. Obama's so cool.
> If you're ever around Michelle, you'll
> Think Nina Simone
> And Paula Poundstone
> And the dance team at the Juilliard School.

The composer P.D.Q. Bach played my show in the early years under the name Peter Schickele, which rhymes with "trickily" and "stickily" but those never led to a limerick and I had to resort to slant rhymes.

There was a musician named Schickele
Who could blow "Finicula, Finiculi"
On a tube of toothpaste,
Which was not in good taste,
Though rather amazing technically.

His greatest feat, though, was a joke:
Posing as one of Bach's folk
And writing cantatas
And funny sonatas—
He earned money from being baroque.

Once in Little Rock, I met Charles Portis, another hero, author of *Norwood* and *True Grit* and my favorite, *Masters of Atlantis,* and while other people carried on learned conversation, I scribbled on a napkin:

My hero the novelist Portis
Does not attempt to exhort us
To be wild and free
But rather to be
Patient and wise like a tortoise.

Constructed of plaster and mortise,
His novels tend to be short as
A tale so it's nice
To read them through twice
And give them a chance to transport us.

Visiting the poet Bill Merwin on Maui, in his weathered green cottage with an open lanai looking out at a forest of palm trees he had planted as seedlings over the decades, I scribbled him a few lines:

The tireless Merwin, W. S.,
Wrote ten thousand poems I guess
In view of the sea

And in each poem a tree
Hiding Eve in a state of undress.

I love Sharon Olds's beautiful erotic poem "Topography" (*"face to face, East to West, my/San Francisco against your New York, your/Fire Island against my Sonoma, my/New Orleans deep in your Texas"*) and once read it onstage at the 92nd Street Y as she sat a few feet away and faintly blushed, one arm folded against her peninsulas, the other arm lying on her delta.

The confessional bard Sharon Olds
Writes explicit work that unfolds
To expose wild nights
And primordial sights
And also small children with colds.

Jim Harrison of Michigan wrote great poetry that is overshadowed by his fame as a novelist. He listened to my radio show that drifted across Lake Superior to his cabin in the Michigan woods.

Jim Harrison of Grayling, Mich.,
Said "Poetry's my favorite dish.
To go out sailing,
Not cling to the railing,
And come home with a poem and a fish."

Mark Twain got rich off *Tom Sawyer* and built an extravagant brick castle in Hartford and made a disastrous investment in the Paige typesetting machine, which kept breaking down, and Twain was forced to close up his mansion and hit the road as a comedy act, traveling around the world to regale foreign audiences, peasants and potentates, mechanics and merchants, with his stories and gags, his set-piece readings from *Huckleberry Finn* and *Life on the Mississippi*. He was funnier than Dickens, who also toured extensively, and his vast success was darkened by the deaths of three of his four children and his wife, Olivia.

Our great humorist Mister Twain
Went broke on the goddam insane
Paige typesetter
And so, as a debtor,
Hit the road to go entertain.

Calcutta to Kalamazoo,
Paris to Park Avenue,
Same old jokes
To different folks,
And wore himself out—wouldn't you?

America's great humorist
Wound up thoroughly pissed
At how his life
Brought grief to his wife,
And much more—in fact, a whole list.

Thank God, we're in a new age
When a man is not forced on the stage
To stand up and speak
Six nights a week
After losing his way on the Paige.

✣ 10 ✣

Birthing

I WROTE A quintuple in December 1997, when Jenny took a taxi to New York-Cornell Hospital on the East River and there brought forth a tiny naked girl who was handed to me by the nurse, a six-pound infant waving her arms, her dark eyes glittering. She passed the Apgar test and was swaddled and put into a bassinet in the nursery.

> The night she came into the world
> I held my own little girl.
> Dark eyes looked at me
> So carefully,
> Her legs and her arms all atwirl.
>
> There were times at 3 a.m.
> She created such utter mayhem,
> With wild alarms
> As she lay in my arms:
> No Christ child, No Bethlehem.
>
> Once at a café she demands
> A taste of blue cheese from France.
> She swallowed and shook

Her head—what a look!
And vomited into my hands.

One day she walked 'cross the floor,
Bare naked, squatted—Good Lord,
And dropped three feces.
I caught all three. She's
The only one I'd do that for.

Scripture says: Except ye be
As children, you shall not see
Paradise, and by a
Daughter named Maia
I've seen it up close happily.

Years later, I did a show in New York and sang duets with Heather Masse who looked like she had a basketball under her blouse. The child, she said, was a girl, due in a month, and she whispered the name, and the next day I wrote the child her first limerick, one with multiple porches.

We're anxious to see Ida Rose
When she emerges and grows
To become who she is,
Perhaps a math whiz
With a novel in front of her nose,
Or gets long and tall
And plays basketball
With a sharp eye and sharper elbows.
She may irritate Heather
By wearing black leather
Jackets and gold pantyhose.
She may irritate Ian
With her love of neon
Lipstick and redneck gun shows.

But inevitably
The child will be
Their girl from her head to her toes.
Spunky and classy,
A Duncan and Masse,
And blessed wherever she goes.

For the singer Aoife O'Donovan who brought forth a child:

It is my hope and belief a
god feels artistic relief a
sort of leitmotif as
with enormous drive he
brings forth an ivy
to lie between eric and aoife.

I saw a terrific soprano, Ellie Dehn, sing the role of the Countess in *The Marriage of Figaro* at the Met and was stunned to see in the program that she's from my hometown of Anoka, Minnesota, so I spent intermission writing:

A soprano named Miss Ellie Dehn
Dyed her hair neon green,
Wound a snake round her head
Because, as she said,
"To be heard, a girl must be seen."

A year later, she sent a photograph of the most beautiful baby ever put on the planet, a tiny thing holding her foot to her mouth, and her eyes—dear Lord, the focus of intellect in those eyes! A gift was called for.

That beautiful brave Arabella
Picked up her foot and could smell a
Delicate rose
That grows in her toes
And she sang O so sweet, a cappella.

I am an elderly fella
With a whiskey and dark panatela
But the smile of Miss A
Makes a sunshiny day,
And I put away my umbrella.

Miss Dehn's motherhood gave me the chance to write her many postcards with limericks, which she stuck to her refrigerator, of which the best was:

The opera star Ellie Dehn
Can do passion like you've never seen,
Can fill up the stage
With horror or rage,
Now she's going for STRONG and SERENE.

A soprano sings from her belly,
But Puccini, Bellini, Ponchielli
Cannot compare
To the child lying there,
The great masterpiece of Miss Ellie.

❧ 11 ❧

Immortality

I WAS MINDING my own business in the Seattle airport, waiting to board a plane to Minnesota, feeling sheepish about my ticket for seat 1B, not wanting fans of mine to see me among the wide-rides up front. I'm a Midwesterner from flat country; I don't seek privilege. My excuse for sitting in 1B is to have more room for writing, but how much space do you need for a limerick? You can write it on an index card.

> I do not belong in First Class,
> In high school, I barely could pass.
> Helen Hunt taught Latin
> And the chair that I sat in
> Was not in front, you bet your ass.

I stood waiting for everyone else to go down the jetway and a woman marched up with a young man in tow. Her son Jared, fifteen. Horn-rims and sandy hair, jean jacket, black tee. He stood beaming while she explained that he was a big fan of my show and had memorized some poems of mine and Jared stepped up, all alert and appropriate, and recited in a bright, clear voice:

> There was a young man from the city
> Who formed a campaign committee

But gave up the race
When he saw that his face
Looked just like his butt, what a pity.

He had memorized it for his tenth-grade speech class, and also:

There was an old lady of Knoxville
Who bought her brassieres by the boxful
Which she stuffed with corn kernels
And old *Wall Street Journals*
To keep the fronts of her frocks full.

And:

There was an attractive stockbroker
Who beat everybody at poker.
Her blouse was revealing
And also concealing
The ace of hearts and the joker.

And:

A young fellow from Pocatello
Said, "Why is my urine bright yellow?
Was it something I ate?
Or could it be Kate
Whom I dated on Saturday?—hello!"

Jared was quite pleased with himself, reciting limericks to their elderly author without a single mistake. I wrote down his address and mailed him a postcard from Minneapolis.

Thanks to the memorable Jared
From a poet up in a garret.
That you memorized
My limericks surprised
Me so much I hardly can bear it.

It's an honor to be quoted. H. L. Mencken assumed he'd be remembered for his scholarly *The American Language* and instead he is remembered for "Nobody ever went broke underestimating the intelligence of the American people." And: "If, after I depart this vale, you ever remember me and have thought to please my ghost, forgive some sinner and wink your eye at some homely girl." He worked hard, year after year, in his upstairs office in his row house on Hollins Street in Baltimore, but God bless him, most of it is uphill reading today, whereas two offhand smart remarks are still quoted. Mark Twain's best work may have been *Innocents Abroad* but his immortality lies in the fact that every day, somewhere in America, people quote him, either "The reports of my death have been greatly exaggerated"; or "I smoke in moderation, only one cigar at a time"; or "I've lived through some terrible things in my life, some of which actually happened." A. J. Liebling wrote gorgeous books but he is remembered for having said, "I can write better than anybody who can write faster, and I can write faster than anybody who can write better."

Being quoted is all the immortality you could want. Rich people try to buy theirs by putting their names on walls. Some poor schnook named David Geffen paid $100 million to have his name carved over the front door of Philharmonic Hall in New York. He didn't realize that nobody looks up as they walk in—concertgoers look down, to avoid tripping on the stairs.

> I'm sorry you spent so much, Dave.
> My gosh, the money you'd save
> If, instead of the portal,
> You'd put your immortal
> Name down below on the pave.
>
> The place where your name should go at
> Is right down on the doormat,
> And as we wipe our feet
> On you, Mr. Elite,
> We'll say "Thank you" and take off our hat.

Rich men donate millions to colleges, hoping to be associated with science and the arts rather than predatory business practices, price-fixing, and influence peddling, but it doesn't work out that way.

> Nobody quotes Rockefeller,
> That crafty old New York cliff dweller,
> And Andrew Mellon
> Was just a rich felon
> And a rather piss-poor storyteller.

> Mr. Bezos, what has he said
> Off the top of his head?
> Or the DuPonts—
> Their speeches—who wants
> To hear them publicly read?

> Henry Ford was a terrible bore.
> Bill Gates? You've heard it before.
> Tell Warren Buffett
> He's said enough, it
> Is late. Good night, there's the door.

I had been a hardworking writer for more than fifty years and written novels, essays, sonnets, sketches, and four decades of a weekly saga of a little town in Minnesota (*It has been a quiet week in Lake Wobegon*). I invented a private eye, Guy Noir (*A dark night in a city that knows how to keep its secrets, but on the twelfth floor of the Acme Building, one man is still trying to find the answers to life's persistent questions.*). But radio is of the moment, like scattering hibiscus blossoms on a pond, like writing with your index finger on a frosty window. Sic transit radio. You're a phenomenon and a national treasure and then the earth turns and you're a guy spilling soup on his shirt.

You wonder now and then: "What am I leaving for posterity?" Well, here was a posterity named Jared and he remembered the lady whose breasts lay in beds of corn and the stockbroker with the ace of hearts and the joker. If that's my legacy, well, okay. The young fellow from Pocatello is good enough for me, and dead men can't be choosers.

✣ **12** ✣

Travels

From Vienna to Prague to New York,
I love those moments my fork
Hits apple strudels,
Gravy and noodles,
Sausage and morsels of pork.

SO I'M IN Vienna and buy three dozen postcards and address them to friends in small towns, friends with little kids, elderly friends, friends who don't travel much—but what to write, other than "Having a big time. Lucky us. Poor you." A limerick of course.

There was an old fellow in Wien
Weary of all the cuisine
Who wanted to gota
St. Cloud, Minnesota,
For a White Castle and Dairy Queen.

There was an old fellow in Wien
Who was feeling ugly and mean
But he'd spent just one term in
Studying German
And none of his Deutsch was obscene.

> There was an old fellow in Wien
> Shocked at the scenes he had seen
> Of religious schism,
> Imperialism,
> And men eating pork, nothing green.

We go on to Prague and a lunch with our former Czech nannies Katerina and Kaya. They were a godsend for us and our fussy baby; they were steady, good-humored, sang to the baby, and the sound of Czech singing comforted her as English could not, and we will be always in their debt. We sat with them under a canopy in a little café on the bank of the Vltava, an idyllic two hours, and it occurs to me, while waiting for the coffee and puff pastry, that I could give them something unique to remember the day by.

> A boisterous lady named Kaya
> Liked to sit down and tie a
> Ribbon of bangles
> To each of her ankles
> And boogie to Handel's *Messiah*.

> There was a young lady named Katja
> Who snuck up on men and cried, "Got ya!"
> They peed in their pants
> And she clapped her hands
> And said, "Look what a lesson I taught ya."

In Prague, we stayed in a hotel looking up at the Castle and down at the Vltava where the lean young actuary Franz Kafka went rowing for exercise. We sat in a park where our little girl ran around joyfully with Czech children and seemed oblivious to any language barrier whatsoever—it was all about smiling and laughing and holding hands and sliding down a slide and swinging on swings—and it struck me how much Franz had missed by not marrying his girlfriend Felice Bauer and starting a family. Fatherhood would have changed him for the better.

Kafka was lonely in Prague
And lived in a neurotic fog,
Groaning and keening
And longing for meaning—
He should've just gotten a dog

And a family. Though no bed of roses,
Children, and wiping their noses,
And keeping them snug
As a bug in a rug,
It's a wonderful metamorphosis.

Children bring merriment, Franz,
Turn sorrows into bygones,
And love Papa Kafka
And suddenly blast off ka-
Pow, as a bright morning dawns.

From Prague to London, where we took a train through Reading where Oscar Wilde had served his time for sodomy and I thought of him touring the U.S. in his green velvet jacket striking aesthetic poses for the miners and journalists, trying to scandalize the upright, reveling in their disapproval.

The aesthete-in-chief Oscar Wilde
Was always exquisitely styled
And witty on cue
And certainly knew
When newspaper stories were filed.

And then he got frisky and fell
And the newspapers covered it well:
Oscar hit bottom, he
Was jailed for sodomy,
"Jail" spelled g-a-o-l.
Others committed a sin

Duplicitously with a grin,
But the love illicit he
Craved was publicity
And that is what did Oscar in.

13

Me and Emily

THE NOBEL PRIZE in Literature will not come my way. I know this. (*Men who write poems that sell are unlikely to win the Nobel and I'd rather peddle than win a gold medal.* Tack så mycket, *Swedes, go to hell.*) But posterity makes its own choices. Many are the medal winners who sank in the swamp of obscurity, while oddballs rose to posthumous fame—Edgar Allan Poe—Thoreau—Emily Dickinson. Legions of her admirers make pilgrimages to her gravesite in Amherst and leave pebbles or poems in homage. My gravesite is out in the middle of nowhere, much harder to find than hers, which is well-marked and in all the guide books. She lived in one house for most of her life where now docents lead tour groups up the stairs to her bedroom. I've lived in several dozen houses: no museum for me. And she lived a simple straightforward life, thanks to remaining single, whereas my life is a tangle of relationships, some of them bewildering even to me. She is so much what I am not—or is it the other way around?—and right there is the basis of my love affair with her, the most famous shy person in American literature, who wrote in a small precise hand dazzling poems, many of them tiny, that I now look at and see were attempting to be limericks. Look at this one:

> *O Wild Nights! were I with* thee.
> *Wild Nights should be our luxury*

95

You've won my heart
It's off the chart.
I wait for you to unbutton me.

She was heading toward limerick, then lost her way.

Because I could not stop for you,
You stopped for me. We rode through
The School in Town
You touched my Gown
And Felt my Flower drenched with Dew.

Emily was a witty and sociable young woman pressed hard by religious bullying, who retreated to her bedroom and garden to write her eggshell poems and live within a small circle of sister Lavinia, brother Austin, and sister-in-law Sue. She reached out to a scholar and critic named Higginson for encouragement, a man who wrote thirty-five books that nobody reads today except out of morbid curiosity. He didn't get Emily. He tried to make her sound more like John Greenleaf Whittier. It's painful for me to read her letters to him, pleading for his support. It should have been me. I understand her. He was clueless.

Dear Emily D. of Amherst
Seldom shouted or cursed
Except when the birds
Dropped little white turds,
She said, "Shit," but that was the worst.

And when Thomas Higginson sneered
At her poems and said they were weird,
She said, "Screw you, Tommy,
With a giant salami!"
And she put chewing gum in his beard.

"Hope is the thing with feathers,"
But she preferred zippers and leathers

And she liked to wear a
Lot of mascara
To Saturday night get-togethers.

Her "Life had stood—a Loaded Gun"—
She kept it hidden in her bun.
And she shot the ass
Off a snake in the grass
And blasted at Stars just for fun.

No one attempted to date her
But it was discovered much later,
The "fly" she heard buzz
In reality was
A little windup hand vibrator.

Whenever she shook someone's hand,
It buzzed and just as she planned,
They let out a shriek
And were dizzy and weak,
And wept and barely could stand.

She said she was crazy for me
And loved me passionately.
"I'm yours," said Emily,
"Let's make a family."
And perhaps we shall, in Eternity.

14

The Necessity
of Limerick Revival

THE AUDIENCE FOR limericks is small, like the audience for hopscotch or Inuktitut poetry. The limerick went out of favor back during the Harding administration in a time of American expansionism and extravagant prosperity and general blather and we need to bring formal verse back to restore a sense of limits. Most poems are too long. A limerick is not.

> I have a good deal to say
> About life in the U.S. today
> And national decline
> But it's the fourth line,
> So I guess I am done now. Okay?

Writing limericks you discover that a story can gain from compression.

> I used to do avant-garde dance
> With a blowtorch, blue paint, and no pants,
> Which some people guessed
> Was genius, and the rest
> Left quickly when given the chance.

I once walked into a hotel in Dallas and saw a big beefy guy walk by, no insignia, carrying a rifle and two pistols in holsters on an ammo belt. A crowded lobby and people around me paid no attention to him. I could've written a 3,000-word essay but instead I wrote:

> There are men—not my problem, but Dallas's—
> Who look upon pistols as phalluses,
> And it makes them feel hot
> To fire a shot
> At the *Journal of Psychoanalysis.*

Once, out walking on a rainy spring morning, I saw a man standing by the roadside, looking down at tiny bodies of frogs splatted on the asphalt. I stopped. He said, looking down, "You'd think there'd be a way they could keep frogs from crossing the road." And there was a limerick there. (I changed "frog" to "toad" because it rhymes with "road.")

> There was an old liberal named Kurt
> Who wore his heart on his shirt.
> The sight of a toad
> Lying crushed on the road
> Left him shaken and visibly hurt.
>
> He empathized hither and yon
> Even while mowing his lawn,
> And whenever he put
> Down his right foot,
> He worried what he had stepped on.
>
> He founded an organization,
> United Amphibian Nation,
> To act as watchdogs
> To protect toads and frogs
> From man's motorized transportation.
>
> Kurt was on guard by a tree,
> Watching frogs swim in the sea.

A stroke of bad luck:
An amphibious truck
Flattened him there. R.I.P.

As I discovered when I was fifteen, the rhymes can lead you down a path you wouldn't have otherwise noticed. Owatonna is a respectable city in southern Minnesota but in limerick form, it recreates itself.

An old Lutheran near Owatonna
Grew ten acres of marijuana.
It went up in a blaze
And for seventeen days
He had visions of the Blessed Madonna.

And the form offers one an exit from the pieties that are imposed on us, pieties that smother generosity of spirit, pieties that lead to self-revulsion.

The limerick's become my obsession,
My favorite mode of confession
Of sins multitudinous,
The lewd and the crude in us,
The most indiscreet indiscretion.

Dirty limericks are a gift to help the overly proprietous such as myself get loose of constraint for a moment. All the great dirty limericks have been written but someone needs to keep the tradition alive and here I am.

In the Little House books, Ma and Pa
Were saintly, without any flaw,
And yet late at night
In dim candlelight
They undressed and saw what they saw.

There was passion out on the prairie
Though discretion was necessary,
The Ingalls weren't singles.

> He beguiled her,
> She got wilder
> In a Little House in the West.
> While Mary slept,
> They undressed
> And cohabited,
> Took a stab at it,
> And they had Laura and Carrie.

I was brought up in a good Christian home, but now and then you need to cross the line in order to ward off sanctimony. I read the rapturous writings of St. John of the Cross, Thomas Merton, Fred Rogers, Oprah Winfrey, my brain goes numb, but when Stan Laurel puts his finger in his mouth and blows and makes his hat rise, or when Oliver Hardy appears in drag, I feel quickened. Or when I recall the young man of Madras.

I still have hopes of writing a dirty limerick that will become a classic like the one about the young couple named Kelly who were found lying belly to belly, but it's a tall order. This is not bad:

> At the nursing home, counting the heads,
> The caregivers giving out meds
> Dispense supersize
> Viagra to guys
> So they don't roll out of their beds.

Men are different from women. My sweet wife loves to look at art, especially the French impressionists and the sunny gardens of Pierre Bonnard. I see no reason to paint flowers. And I believe that abstract expressionism is for the lobbies of large insurance companies. The true calling of an artist is to confront the naked female form. That's what separates the true artists from the wallpaper-hangers.

> Chopin wrote a lovely étude
> That, when performed in the nude
> By a mademoiselle

Who plays fairly well,
Can certainly uplift the mood.

We must strive for a workable plan
That benefits woman and man
For everyone's sake it—
Good Lord, is she naked?
And isn't that lovely Chopin?

I am thinking of that lovely Étude, Op. 10, No. 3 ("Tristesse") that I heard
as a boy sung by Jo Stafford on the radio. It was radio so I don't know if she
was naked or not. It was entirely up to her whether to take off her clothes
or not, but if she had, and I were in the studio, I would have looked.
Glanced. Sidelong, but still.

Let's listen to jazz—Charles Mingus—
And I will perform cunnilingus
And give you some head
As you lie there in bed
And see what delight it will bring us.

"Lay" is a transitive verb.
It takes an object, like "herb,"
Or maybe a maid
If she'd like to be laid,
And there's no sign: *Do Not Disturb*.

If I were twenty-five, I wouldn't publish that limerick for fear of offending
important people who might deny my child admission to a good college,
but I'm an old man now and no longer dependent on public approval
and anyway my daughter is done with college and going on to real life.

15

Limericks of Lit

I grant you it's good to be real
And to hear how troubled souls feel
That the dark is immense,
But friends don't let friends
Go alone to see Eugene O'Neill.

THE ENGLISH DEPARTMENT looked at light verse as a childish bad habit like playing trombone. (Cello or violin, yes. Guitar, okay. Trombone, no.) Our professors herded us into large airless rooms to pore over Wordsworth and Coleridge and Byron, for whom five lines was only a burp, who needed at least five hundred for a walk around the block. I thought of Wordsworth years later while lying under a sheet on a cushiony massage table, aromatic candles burning, bamboo flute music playing, and it struck me that the holistics industry came from the Romantics, that it's not about musculature and stress, it's about redemption.

A poet named Wordsworth, old Bill
Liked to climb to the top of a hill
And sit spellbound for hours
Looking at flowers
This was years before movies, but still.

Bill Wordsworth beheld Tintern Abbey
And it made him holistically happy
And filled with such awe
He opened a spa
And soon he was crazy and crabby.

In dealing with anxious spa patients,
He lost all of his intimations
Of immortality
To the sheer banality
Of health spa administration.

Welcome to the club, Mr. W.
You start out chasing a bubble, you
Follow your dream
Of a transcendent scheme
And the details descend to trouble you.

Don't leap up when you behold
A rainbow and look for the gold.
Natural piety
Can turn to anxiety:
And revelations should not be sold.

Melville's stock was high at the time and I tried to read him and never got far.

I never could read *Moby-Dick*
And not only because it's so thick
But the trip *to* the ship
Is a slow drip-drip
And the whale won't appear
For about half a year,
So I think I will wait for the flick.

Obviously I did not get a good education at the University of Minnesota and it was my own fault. I was in dread of becoming an academic and having to teach for a living and the best insurance against that was to do poorly in school, so I did. Humor and ignorance go hand in hand: I was pretty sure about that. I fully intended to be a humorist and so devised:

AN ABECEDARY OF LITERARY ABSURDITY

Miss Austen, the valiant Jane,
Abstained from gin and cocaine
And consorting with men,
But now and again
She was thrilled to take walks in the rain.

The grim satirist Ambrose Bierce
Made fun of mankind something fierce
And he disappeared
And, what is so weird,
Returned as a girl, Mildred Pierce.

The Beat poet Gregory Corso
Sang out and thumped on his torso.
He was boyish and sweet
And light on his feet
Like Allen Ginsberg but more so.

The author James Fenimore Cooper
Wrote himself into a stupor,
Weekdays and weekends,
Natty Bumppo, Mohicans:
Good writer but big party pooper.

Teenagers love E. E. Cummings
For his romantic hummings and strummings
And his embrace

Of The All-Lower Case
And he didn't write long but short, Cummings.

The debut of Theodore Dreiser,
Sister Carrie, came up like a geyser,
And trying to match it he
Wrote *American Tragedy,*
Which was stronger, sadder, and wiser.

Tommy (Mr. Eliot, T. S.)
Never ate peaches, I guess,
Or rolled up his pants
Or had a romance
Except with a sense of distress.
We read *Alfred Prufrock* in school,
So dry, and like April, so cruel,
And we wrote in its praise
Like it was beef fillets
Instead of a cold chicken gruel.

Poor old Fitzgerald, F. Scott,
Started out famous, red-hot,
Got drunk at the Plaza,
Imagined that he was a
Hemingway, but he was not.

An Ohio dentist, Zane Grey,
Wrote Westerns, yippee-i-ay,
Today he's not read,
We have TV instead,
But he's dead so I'm sure it's okay.

The anthem by Julia Ward Howe,
When sung by a massed choir—wow.
The Lord's judgment seat,

The jubilant feet,
I wish we could hear it right now.

The letter I, naturally,
Is meant to represent me.
The writer, myself,
My books on your shelf,
My voice speaking sensitively.

Henry James preferred the obscure,
The elaborate scenic detour—
You say, "Coffee or tea?"
He replies lengthily—
Yes or no? You cannot be sure.

That farmer girl Miss Maxine Kumin
Set out to praise and illumine.
And ruminate
On things small and great
And the bond between landscape and human.

A troubled man, Robert Lowell,
Was bipolar deep in his soul,
And despite his great gifts,
He worked double shifts
Deep in the mine digging coal.

Edna St. Vincent Millay
Was a love goddess back in the day,
Green eyes and red hair
And bohemian flair.
She tangled with men
And girls now and then,
Which gave her plenty to say.
After many affairs,

She slipped on the stairs,
And died, which is not the worst way.

A formalist, Nemerov (Howard),
Believed that a poem is powered
By attention to time,
Space, rhythm and rhyme,
That free verse is the work of a coward.

The novelist Joyce Carol Oates
Writes books like others write notes.
A hundred pages
An hour—outrageous—
It flows out of her as she floats.

The poet of life Mary Oliver
Every day harked to the call of her
Flowers and birds
And put into words
The entirety, everything, all of her.

Dear devout Flannery O'Connor
Well knew that she was a goner,
Sat down and wrote stories
Of desperate glories
As the good Lord smiled down on her.

To the dashing young blade Frank O'Hara,
New York was the French Riviera,
The rain on the pavement,
The looks that he gave men
And wished for a much gayer era.

Edgar (Weird Ed) Allan Poe
Lost his Lenore long ago
And Annabel Lee

So no wonder he
Heard a raven—or was it Old Crow?

Question: are limericks art,
Possessing a soul and a heart,
Or simply the smile
Of innocent guile
After a small pungent fart?

The great satirist Philip Roth
Wrote comedy out of whole cloth,
Combining the Yiddish
With tragic and skittish,
But sustaining, like hot chicken broth.

Gertrude Stein Gertrude Stein Gertie
Is not so heavy but sturdy
Where she is she is there
With birds in her hair
Well-girded and wonderfully wordy.

The great transcendental Thoreau
Went to live in the woods long ago
And wrote lovely prose
While his mom washed his clothes
And fixed him hot lunches to go.

The prodigious productive Updike
Wrote prose like riding a bike,
Fiction, reviews,
Verse to amuse,
Throwing strike after strike after strike.

Gore was in love with Vidal,
The gentleman who had it all,
Intelligence, style,

Great books, a whole pile—
If you doubt it, give him a call.

Tennessee Williams could tell a
Story in play or novella
And made a rough fella
Kowalski to yell a
Wonderful classic line: "Stella!"

The poet X. J. (Joe) Kennedy,
In Ireland, would be in the Senate. He
Is up there with Yeats,
But here in the States,
A poet is a minor amenity.

Y, my dear reader, is You,
Without whom whatever we do
Has little meaning
Like a tree that is leaning
And falls in the woods out of view.

And Z is for zest and pizzazz,
Which all great literature has,
The song and the beat
Of feet in the street,
The juice and the joy and the jazz.

16

Light Verse on Dark Subjects

THE LIMERICK'S LOW reputation is due partly to its brevity but also to its reputation for silliness, so the veteran limericist feels obligated to show that limericks can walk on the dark side of the street. It dawned on me that nobody had written limericks about suicides, and why not? An excess of delicacy, if you ask me. Just because a person chooses to expel him/herself from the world does not mean we should put them permanently behind a dark curtain. So I set out to correct this lapse.

> Hart Crane was somewhat arcane
> And wrote in a modernist vein.
> His poem "The Bridge"
> Is not taped to my fridge
> For reasons I need not explain.

> Virginia Woolf walked out alone,
> Her pockets loaded with stone,
> To the River Ouse
> After years of sad news,
> She found a room of her own.

> Hemingway wound up his journey
> In a long depressing downturn—he

Picked up a gun
As his father had done,
And they wrapped Ernie up on a gurney.

Poor dear Sylvia Plath
Was torn up by sorrow and wrath
The day that she dove
Headfirst in the stove,
She should have just run a hot bath.

Mr. Thompson, the great Hunter S.,
Faced the classic distress
Of being eleven
When you're sixty-seven,
Decided his life was a mess,
Painful, insane,
So he blew up his brain
And everything went blank, I guess.
He was vulgar, literate, loud,
A son of the old Grub Street crowd,
A hunter of frauds,
Fakers, false gods.
He crashed but the man never bowed.

Vincent pursued his rainbow
With roses and meadow in tow
And painted like mad
And gave all he had
To give and then Vincent let gogh.

Mark Antony, widely adored,
Gained power but then he got bored
And in search of the *neo-*
He took up with Cleo,
Was beaten and fell on his sword.

The poet, the sexy Anne Sexton
Created some elegant text in
The midst of her madness
And wild with gladness
She flew and then crashed in dejection.

The whimsicalist Richard Brautigan
Set out one day to see God again
And picked up a gun
And thought, "Am I done?"
And shot and therefore never thought again.

Poor old D. Foster Wallace
Whose writings offer no solace,
But unnerve and depress
With successful excess,
Literature terminalis.

Basquiat, the poor son of a bitch,
Died young of heroin, which
Meant a work of his sold
For a truckload of gold,
A hell of a way to get rich.

The beautiful Marilyn Monroe
Performed all her life as a show,
Then took barbiturates:
Sadder but richer, it's
How those storylines go.

Others who'd given up hope
Died at the end of a rope,
Or, weeping and weary,
Performed hara-kiri,
Or swallowed a handful of dope.

If I were to do myself in,
From remorse at the jerk I had been,
I might use a noose
Or I might choose
To reform by confessing my sin.

And then I thought of my friend and classmate Corinne Guntzel whose grave in Crystal Lake Cemetery I've visited often. She was buried there in the spring of 1986. She was forty-three. I had seen her the summer before at the twenty-fifth anniversary reunion of our high school graduating class, buoyant as ever, a girl I'd known since the first grade. We walked to grade school together on foggy fall mornings, careful to walk on the shoulder on the left side, facing oncoming traffic, and up ahead the shouts of classmates on the playground, playing kickball. I flew out to Seneca Falls when I heard about her death and got there in time for an impromptu memorial at Wells College where she taught economics, the room packed with weeping students. She had climbed into a canoe late one night with her jacket pockets filled with rocks and paddled out to the middle and tipped the boat over and drowned. At the funeral in Minneapolis, I could not bring myself to walk up front to view her body and so I sat in back with a pad of paper and scribbled some lines.

Here's to my classmate Corinne
With whom I was tempted to sin
And be wild and obscene
When we were eighteen
And now it's too late to begin.

Why didn't we neck in the car
Or swim naked off the sandbar?
We had many chances
At parties and dances
And yet remained chaste. How bizarre.

> Now my beauty lies in her grave,
> Alone in a dark musty cave.
> O let it be known,
> Children, do not postpone
> Adventure. Rise up. Misbehave.

Her old parents, Hilmer and Helen, stood paralyzed with grief, stolid, un-weeping, brokenhearted. And there I stood by the gravesite as a Methodist minister read the resurrection chapter from First Corinthians. Now the three of them lie in that grave, under a stone that tells the barest facts. Every time I drive north on I-94 and pass the exit that would take me to the cemetery, I think of her and the mystery of her death.

> Time, that old thief, brings us grief
> And the years and seasons are brief
> But still if we treasure
> The days in full measure
> We cross the barrier reef
> And enter the ocean
> Of endless devotion
> Depending upon your belief.

❧ 17 ❧

Don't Forget Flatulence, of Course

The Beatles said all that you need
Is love, which is lovely indeed,
And I don't take issue
And yet toilet tissue
Is useful, too, one must concede.

THE THREE STAGES of writing: You start out wanting to be considered brilliant, and then you want to be paid for your work, extravagantly if possible, and in the final stage, which I'm in, you want to be useful. This is the beauty of the limerick. It's easy to seem brilliant—just be incomprehensible and go on from there—but a limerick that makes people laugh is a useful thing. After the following limerick, a man wrote to me, "I thought that only happened to me." No, sir. It is universal.

Sex! What a thrilling occasion!
The joy of intense exaltation!
And then in the dark
You hear spiders bark
And lift up the sheet—ventilation.

There was a young flutist named Keith,
Who was given the champion's wreath,

Playing duets by Schütz
On the flute, with bass toots
From the embouchure down underneath.

There was a trombonist named Vicky
Whose keys were twisted and tricky,
Her slide was bad, too,
And the note, when she blew,
Was brownish, smelly, and sticky.

There was an old fart from Anoka
Made a stink so strong it could choke a
Horse—loud reports
Came out of his shorts
And the smell was not like tapioca.

The Vulgar Limerick is an ancient tradition. The best ones have been written by Anon, long ago. But it's a limericist's duty to keep trying to add to the treasury, and I do, and I shall. Just this morning I awoke at 6, formulated the following, and wrote it down.

Masculine monks of Manassas
Sat passing gas during Masses.
The musical tones
Were like massive trombones
And the smell was like musky molasses.

Flatulence seldom appears in serious fiction, which is hard to believe—*naturalism* without the expulsion of gas?—and you won't find it in Walt Whitman, gassy though he is, but it is very much at home in the limerick, especially ones written by old men like me.

An old baritone, Jeremiah,
Farted during Handel's *Messiah*
And the blast from his ass

Ignited the brass
And they played the rest half a step hiah.

And one for my daughter who enjoys flatulence almost as much as I do.

Blessed the papa, or *Vater*,
Who has himself a good daughter
Who, though she is older,
Puts her head on his shoulder,
And laughs at his jokes, as he's taught her.
O lucky the daddy, or *père*,
Whose daughter is sitting right there,
Attentive and sweet
As she tickles his feet
And he farts but she doesn't care.

I'm unreasonably proud of the next limerick, about the great Swedish soprano. A limerick with an opera star *and* flatulence sets you apart from the crowd.

The sweet nightingale Jenny Lind
Walked down the street breaking wind.
Beautifully dressed
But everyone guessed
It was her by the way that she grinned.

I once sang a duet with Heather Masse and passed gas in the middle of it. It's not possible to sing open-throated and keep the sphincter clamped shut and so there we were singing about starlight and dewdrops and sounds of the rude world, and suddenly there was one. This is nothing I'd mention in a memoir but it fits perfectly into a book of limericks.

"Beautiful dreamer, queen of my heart,"
I sang with Heather and then let a fart.
It was a low D

And it came out of me
Though we were but two feet apart.

Heather's a peach and a pro
And we went on with the show
And we sang the refrain
Amongst the methane
As it settled down in the front row.

Two months later, Miss Masse
Asked me to lunch (she's so classy).
I sat and was pushin'
A small whoopee cushion
That sounded vulgar and gassy.

She chortled and held up her thumbs
And grinned with her teeth and her gums
And whinnied and wheezed
And was thoroughly pleased
And ever since then we've been chums.

That is the truth. The woman invited me to lunch at a ritzy café. She arrived early and placed a whoopee cushion on the chair opposite her. I saw it and, without a word, sat down on it hard, as a gentleman should do when a woman goes to all that trouble, and it sounded like the mating call of a bull elephant and she went to pieces. I even feigned shock and embarrassment. It was wonderful. I may be wrong but it seems to me that with the decline in popularity of the whoopee cushion, the dribble glass, the handshake buzzer, etc., has come a rising tide of anxiety, depression, obsessive behavior, etc., and is this only a coincidence? You tell me.

I'm seventy-seven, I'm sure,
So why am I so immature?
I am and I know it,

I am a poet
Of farting and the smell of manure.

I feel that you do not truly know someone as a human being until the two of you have passed gas in each other's presence. I am particularly a fan of the farting of mature women. Women who dress up when they go shopping, whose subjects and verbs are always in agreement, who would never utter the word "fart" and who would never be seen reading a book of limericks—nonetheless, body chemistry works the same in them as in the truck driver or the forklift operator and they feel pressure building in the lower tract and they clamp down on the sphincter but it doesn't always work and so, instead of a soft whistle they emit a deep organ note. Once in a fancy café, W.A. Frost, in St. Paul, while I was waiting for a friend to join me for lunch, a matronly woman sat at a nearby table and stared at me and then—

Limericks come easily to me
In moments when, as now, I see
Somebody's aunt
In a lunch restaurant
Smile and fart quietly.

The smile says, "Oh! Was that you?"
But I know that she knows that I knew
And then she arose
To straighten her clothes
And fired off round No. 2.

She jumps up and runs to the john
And waits for me to be gone
And I slowly compose
These lines and then close
My notebook and slowly move on.

A fart is not vulgar or lewd,
No need for contrition, Gertrude.
It is just the expression
Of gassy compression
That comes from digestion of food.

Enjoy your flatulence, dear.
The booms that come from your rear,
They smell corrupt
When they erupt
But it's proof you're alive and you're here.

❧ 18 ❧

Limericks of Love

MY LIMERICK CAREER revived when I met Jenny Nilsson and fell in love, sitting at lunch in a café. She lived near me in New York, a freelance violinist from my hometown of Anoka. Her sister Elsa was a friend of my sister Linda, and she knew my cousin Rebecca, and there we were in the big city, five minutes apart. I called her up and she was friendly but said she was leaving the next day on a concert tour of Asia, which sounded like the truth, not like a rejection. So I waited three months, called back, we had lunch together, and it lasted for three hours. I wrote her a limerick on a napkin, something about "bright as a penny" and "her faults were few, just one or two, and her virtues were lavish and many."

She loved playing music and I courted her by taking her to concerts. And sat beside her and wrote little verses.

> The phenomenal Ludwig Beethoven
> Was in the mood so he dove in,
> Wrote the *Moonlight Sonata*
> And he and his mom got a
> Flat with an icebox and stove in.

Mozart wrote divertimenti,

Fifteen, I'd say, maybe twenty.

They all sound the same,

Rather light, very tame,

I've heard two or three and that's plenty.

Schubert wrote beautiful lieder

But wanted to write for the theater.

It's a great classic tale: your

Fine sense of failure

Makes your song sweeter and sweeter.

At the concert of works by Chas. Ives

Sat well-bred husbands and wives,

And some were deflated,

And some nauseated,

And the others feared for their lives.

She liked seeing concerts from the balcony, rather than the pit, and she was charmed to be romanced by a man who wrote limericks. So I kept on.

There was a composer named Schoenberg

Grew up in a suburb called Fernburg.

He composed in C major

Works about nature

And then he discovered dissonance.

On her freelance earnings, she couldn't afford to go to the opera so I took her out to see *Der Rosenkavalier* with Renée Fleming at the Met.

The opera diva Miss Fleming,

Without any hawing or hemming,

Is the best Marschallin

Between Ho Chi Minh

City and eastern Ishpeming.

And she came to *A Prairie Home Companion* where I had taken care to book more artists I knew she'd adore rather than those she wouldn't. Yes, it's true. To win the heart of a woman, I steered the show away from gutbucket blues and raunch and cowboy yodeling and onto a higher plateau.

> The cellist they call Yo-Yo Ma
> Played Bach on the musical saw.
> After which, for a laugh,
> He cut in half
> A lady in pink pants and bra.

> The mezzo named Marilyn Horne,
> Whose voice with such passion was torn,
> Did *Aida* once
> And after nine months,
> Forty-two babies were born.

> The guitarist Isbin of Sharon
> Performed on the Isle of Aran
> And fired two rockets
> In honor of Bach. It's
> His G-string and Air she was wearin'.

> The banjoist Joseph Newberry
> Makes a sound that easily can carry
> Through windows and doors
> And the sheer sonic force
> Turns milk into cheese at the dairy.

> The violinist Steve Copes
> Plays in the band with high hopes
> That the woodwinds
> Repent of their sins
> And all of the strings learn the ropes.

She was smart, having survived in the music cosmos, enjoying the comradeship, sometimes living on no money, her only amusement a long walk around town, enjoying the odd characters and their phraseology. She spoke well. Thank goodness, I did, too.

> Jenny was sweet as could be
> And I loved her passionately.
> But she said goodbye—
> Bad grammar was why—
> 'Stead of "We" I said, "Her and me."

But I didn't say that and here we are, years later. There are days when I look at her and hear choirs humming Alleluias and there are days when she looks at me and wonders, "Who is he and what is his stuff doing in my house?" Those are the days when I'm glad to leave home and go give a speech somewhere

> Three days without my wife, Jenny
> Is two-point-seven too many.
> Without her, I'm senseless,
> Deaf and defenseless,
> A grasshopper with no antennae.

> And so I simply must tell
> My darling mademoiselle:
> That I hope she can see
> That wherever she
> Is I would be there as well.

Then I fly home and there is my elegant wife waiting for me at Baggage Claim. She puts her arms around me and says, "I missed you." I hand her my limerick.

> My darling can play the viola
> At the same time as she can roll a
> Smoke, tell a joke,

Swim a stroke, drink a Coke
Or as some folks would say, *Coca-Cola.*

She married me when I was a big shot and stuck with me through my long slide into genteel obscurity as my elderly fans have gone off into assisted living and the world is now ruled by millennials. I looked at the list of talent for a Minneapolis summer music festival and *did not recognize the name of one performer.* I read the obits page and young people my age are appearing there.

I opened the VIP gate
And the man said, "Sorry, too late.
You once were VI
In days gone by,
Now you're just P. Beat it, mate."

And Jenny stepped up and said, "He
Is terribly VI to me."
And she decked the guy
With a poke in the eye
And I walked in the men's room to pee.

19

A Very Clear Dream

THE LIMERICK DID not desert me when I hit a big bump in June 2001, while winding up the *Prairie Home* season at Tanglewood. I felt breathless onstage, to the point that I could hardly climb a short flight of stairs without panting. So I parked myself onstage just behind the Shoe Band, caught my breath, and spoke the News from Lake Wobegon slowly to avoid gasping and wheezing that might alarm the radio audience. Jenny was alarmed and called my cousin Dr. Dan and two days later I presented myself at the Mayo Clinic, where Dr. Rodysill listened to my heart briefly and said the words, "Mitral valve prolapse." Soon after, a heart surgeon, Dr. Michael Orszulak, appeared, listened, and told me I had a simple choice: either undergo open-heart surgery to repair the valve or else go home and sit in a sunny corner and wait for the angels to gather me home. It was a large moment for a fifty-nine-year-old who'd been twenty-nine for thirty years. It was a hereditary glitch that no doubt I'd complicated by doing all the tobacco and alcohol a person could do and still remain standing, and it didn't take much deliberation to sign up for surgery. I liked Dr. Orszulak. We talked and I found out he was a steelworker's son from Pittsburgh, first one in the family to go to college, that he loved motorcycles and fly-fishing and he tied his own flies. A man with a sense of caution and good manual skills. So I signed my name on the forms. My wife, Jenny, needed me, as did my little daughter and I felt surrounded by serious competence at Mayo.

> I look at myself in a mirror
> And shudder. It couldn't be clearer.
> I'm old and weary
> And the love of my dearie
> Is suddenly terribly dearer.

I came home for two days, to put my desk in order and throw away *Co-Eds On Spring Break* and *Girls' Shower Room Gala* and other trashy things I wouldn't want my heirs to have to deal with. I went to Walgreens for a powerful prescription laxative, and there stood a woman telling a friend, "He went in to the hospital yesterday and he was eating his supper and then he died. I don't get it." She didn't seem grief-stricken, just uncomprehending. Me, too. Death seemed so inappropriate. A person has better things to do than collapse.

Back to the hospital, I lay in bed, and an orderly shaved my groin for surgery in the morning. I asked him what he'd done in his previous line of work and he said he'd been a farmer. "Sheep?" I said. "Hogs," he said. Jenny and I sat and held hands in silence, then she went home to comfort our little girl, who was worried about her dad. I declined a sleeping pill. I wanted to think a few clear thoughts.

> It's been an interesting drive:
> Thank you that I am alive,
> My Lord and Friend,
> And if it's the end,
> What a good place to arrive.

> Thirty-two was good—forty-three,
> And fifty-five turned out to be.
> On 12/29
> When that daughter of mine
> Was born in living 3-D.

I look back at middle-aged me
And don't always like what I see—
Complacent, stone-faced,
Hung up on good taste,
And rank superiority.

And now at age fifty-nine,
You've sent a very clear sign:
A valve in my heart
Is falling apart,
And I just want a little more time.

Every day is a beautiful gift,
Tender and precious and swift.
The light and the sound,
The sky and the ground,
Every hour cries out to be lived.

Though I may be over the hill,
Still I think I can and I will.
I've forgotten just what
I can and will, but
They remain a goal of mine still.

Every year I pass the date
When my balloon shall deflate.
My mom entered heaven
At ninety-seven,
And I aim to reach ninety-eight.

But if the shadows should fall
Tomorrow and I get the call,
I hope to have time
To speak one last line:
Thank you, Lord. Thanks for it all.

In the morning I was wheeled into the OR and hoisted onto a glassy table in dim bluish light, a crowd of figures in blue around me. Everything so purposeful—no wasted motion, no casual talk, no hesitation, a palpable respect for the mystery of humanity, a powerful sense of smart people united in action to give me back my life—and then the lights went out.

> To the ICU from the OR
> And I thought of "Crossing the Bar"
> But awoke and my boat,
> Though adrift, was afloat.
> "Is it me?" I said. They said: "You are."

I emerged from the mists and lay in the ICU tended for twenty-four hours by three nurses working in shifts, Erin and Erin and Cliff, and managed to write:

> Blessings on you, Dr. Orszulak,
> And if it is only a horse you lack,
> Or a horse and a cart,
> Thanks from my heart,
> Many thanks and also of course a plaque.

Not a great limerick, but not bad for a sedated man.

I had a dream a night or two later, while still in the hospital, in which I was visited by a Japanese warrior bearing a shield and sword, wearing a helmet carved from wood. He informed me that the secret of good health is devotion to art. He said that three arts—poetry, pottery, and archery—if practiced to perfection can ward off all illness and infirmity. He recommended poetry to me. And then he ran away over the hills. And in the morning, I wrote a limerick to the doctor who had seen me through the experience, though his Norwegian last name was a challenge. A small thankyou offering that gives a moment's pleasure, takes up no space, and is easily recycled.

> My physician, good Dr. Rodysill,
> Believes that carelessness rode us ill

And that a brisk walk,
Half an hour by the clock,
Will help, just as us taking notice will.

Notice the stars in the murk,
The medicinal value of work.
Avoid pointless journeys,
Doctors, attorneys,
Be happy, says Rodysill (Kirk).

Encounters with professional expertise are humbling for me. I'd been crazy ambitious—a Minnesota misfit aiming to be a New York slicker and a radio star—and after having my life saved by kind men and women at Mayo, I felt new fondness for the humble limerick. Limericks gave me pleasure and ambition did not. I went back to Mayo with urinary problems that were neatly solved by a woman surgeon who'd mastered a new noninvasive laser method. I trusted her without a scintilla of doubt and I lay in Recovery and wrote her a souvenir:

For the fabulous fair Dr. Krambeck
I could write a poem in iambic,
Compose a toccata
Or a large enchilada
Or sculpt her two hands in ceramic.

A surgeon, first-class, Dr. K
Does amazing things ten times a day,
Reducing the weights
Of enlarged prostates
Without interfering with play.

Years later, I was writing on a legal pad on my lap when Dr. Fulgham, my neurologist, came in my room the day after I'd had a stroke, and he glanced at the pad, curious as to what sort of marmoset gambrel jackass molasses gibberish might be there, but I had written:

Two blood clots up in my brain
Like crooks on the evening train
Who take a room
In the Hotel of Doom
Overlooking the bank on West Main.

They sit peering out through the blinds
With larceny much on their minds
And opening the door
To the safe and cash drawer
And the treasures within that one finds.

When a guy with a mighty ker-blam
Knocks their door off the doorjamb,
It is a blood thinner
Who had spinach for dinner
And he collars both blood clots, *Hot damn!*

Thus Virtue wins out once again,
As the Lone Ranger did way back when,
And thus the alliance
Of kindness and science
Has served me well. Thank you. Amen.

"How are you doing today?" Dr. Fulgham asked. "Never better," I said. A major life event for an old man, clouds of dread, then by God's grace an all-clear, the prescription of a blood thinner, a good prognosis, the patient is dismissed, and discovers that Folks With Strokes Can Still Tell Jokes.

I trust my neurologist Jim
Who fixed my brain, which was dim.
He blew in my ear,
Stuck a pin in my rear,
And I felt tingling in every limb.

I cried, "My good man, bless your heart.

I'm suddenly terribly smart.

One pill from the bottle,

Now I read Aristotle

And I think I am René Descartes."

I wrote one for Dr. Murphy who performed an excellent hemorrhoidectomy when I was in my early thirties, the surgical procedure that dares not say its name but that saved the life of a man who sits at a desk for a living. I was very grateful.

Dermatologists must have good skin.

Dietitians ought to be thin.

And psychiatrists

Have no scars on their wrists,

And proctologists—where to begin?

My daughter Maia, who has Angelman syndrome, was so lucky to find people at Boston Children's Hospital who are studying this rare chromosomal puzzle, and I sat in the corner of Dr. Tan's office and wrote in tribute:

Our man Dr. Wen-Hann Tan

Welcomes the special-needs clan

To his clinic in Boston

The young tempest-tossed in

Their chaos and also élan—

And the spirit at home

Within the syndrome,

The humor, the will, the *I can*

Not seen in statistics

But only by mystics

Like him, an angelic man.

I'm proud of this limerick, written on the spot, in tribute to a great man sitting across the room who, though dedicated to science, appreciates my daughter's comic sensibility. The form of the limerick, likewise, imposes a comic sense on the facts. Such a simple transaction: I am grateful he puts his expertise and humanity at the service of one I love, I write him a limerick and hand it to him, he is touched. Blue Cross doesn't do limericks. I've made his day. My pleasure.

20

Perversity

> A sweet Dvořák serenade
> Is a tender melodic parade
> And yet one can yearn
> For a crash and a burn,
> Sirens and police barricade.

IT IS A PERVERSION, I know, but when I sit in the concert hall listening devoutly to classical music, I feel an urge to pull out a pen and write something unseemly. I used to be an announcer at a classical music station and maybe that dissipated the reverence that one ought to feel as the orchestra plays the Brandenburg No. 1. I hear it and I try to think of a rhyme for "Brandenburg."

> A lewd violinist named Dean
> Played Bach so it sounded obscene
> And his Brandenburg
> Seduced Sandy Berg
> Who was two months short of eighteen.
> She was pure, and to keep her mind clean,
> Although she knew it was mean

She oiled his bow
With Astroglide so
He couldn't be heard, only seen.

I was booked to do a concert with the New York Philharmonic for my seventieth birthday, Rob Fisher conducting, and in gratitude to the players I wrote two dozen limericks for them, which I think they liked—orchestra players are trained not to laugh onstage, however, so they didn't, but they were amused. Itzhak Perlman had never written them a limerick, nor Murray Perahia.

There is a violist named Phelps
Who lives on a diet of kelps
And tofu and berries
Although this varies
And sometimes a martini helps.

There was an old master named Drucker
Who said, "When I'm losing my pucker,
I'll retire, no sweat,
Take my clarinet,
Go on eBay and wait for a sucker."

The trumpet player Phil Smith
Is particular who he hangs with:
He is partial to oboes
And grizzled old hoboes
And girls who belong to B'nai B'rith.

There was a horn player named Myers
Who gave up all earthly desires
To practice and study
Till his lips were bloody
And his arms were held up by two wires.

And then the limerick *de résistance,* for the gentleman in the front corner chair.

> A great violinist, Glenn Dicterow,
> A prince of a man and a victor, O
> He's slicker and quicker
> Than an old-time cornpicker
> Who went with a sack and just picked a row.

And for a nice man in the back row, whose name is also a challenge:

> There is a bass player named Matthew
> Said: "It's easy as taking a bath, you
> Step on the mat,
> Play slightly flat,
> You need a strong grip,
> Some musicianship,
> And if you go down that path, you
> Be manly and crisp,
> Speak up, do not lisp,
> Don't mispronounce *cashew* as *cathew.*"

"Thanks," he said. The limerick wore me out. It was harder than the performance. Too much work for no return. but the name "Mathew" is hard to resist. Next up: Malachi.

21

Permanence

Images flash on the screens,
Hundreds of electric scenes,
Zoom and explode,
Sheer overload—
The fascination
Of mystification
At beautiful faces
In great empty spaces.
Who knows what all of it means?

I CAME OF AGE in a simpler time when a kid might amuse himself for hours with just pencil and paper. "Simplicity, simplicity, simplicity!" said Thoreau. "Let your affairs be as two or three ... and keep your accounts on your thumbnail." That's the limerick: a thumbnail. I write on my thumbnail.

The honest respect of a friend
Is good enough. So defend
Against lavish praise
To the end of your days:
They can eulogize you at the end.

When I want an opinion about a limerick, I hand it to my wife. If she laughs, that's all I need to know. If she is silent and then says, "What is Schlitz?" I know I need to fix it.

> There was a young man who loved Schlitz,
> Which he drank in his room at the Ritz
> With pâté (very rich)
> And olives from which
> His servants had cut out the pits.

Limericks are susceptible to the ravages of time. The Schlitz limerick was a waste of time and also the one about the old man who loved Pabst and drank it until he collapsed and a man who loved Blatz and drank it straight out of the vats along with a platter of vegetable matter and another of animal fats. These brands of beer belong to the past, and besides, my wife is a wine drinker. The world moves on. In 2028, if someone picks up this book, they'll say, "Who is David Geffen?" They'll know who Charles Mingus was, but what was *A Prairie Home Companion*? And who is this guy?

> Vermont is rocky and hilly,
> The people survive willy-nilly,
> The road meanders
> Like Bernie Sanders:
> He'll never be president, will he.

So the limericist goes for place names. Celebrities come and go like butterflies in summer, but Nantucket will always be there. And Elvis's hometown of Tupelo, Mississippi. There is a challenge worthy of the effort. A limerick about Duluth leads you inevitably to *youth* and *truth* and New York to *pork* and *torque* but Tupelo leads you into fresh new territory. As does Chattanooga and Macalester and Boise and Memphis.

> At the big spelling bee in Tupelo
> I misspelled cupola *cupolo*
> And missed out on first prize,

A bedspread, king-size,
With your choice of a red or a blue pillow.

A gentleman from Chattanooga
Loved to fix greens with arugu-
La along with grits
With truffle bits
And maybe a side of beluga.

In Egypt, a girl from Macalester
Found a mummy all dried-up and calloused, her
Hand touched its feet
And under the sheet
She saw its petrified phallus stir.

In Boise, they follow the laws,
Believe that effects have a cause,
Try to do right,
And sometimes at night
They pronounce the name properly: Boise.

A bombastic woman of Memphis
Liked to holler and yell for emphas-
Is and if we choose
She does know the blues
And would be glad to sing them f' us.

Admit it. It's a terrific Memphis limerick. (Nashville is impossible unless you rhyme it with "bashful," which I refuse to do.) And the Macalester one was a high-water mark in the annals of rhyme, which nobody cares about anymore except you and me and two other people. But listen to this—George Latimer was mayor of St. Paul, and if he were from St. Paul, I would've said he's in love with fall when the colors are gorgeous he sits on porches as the flocks of wild geese call, but no, he's from Schenectady.

George Latimer was well-connected, he
Dropped his cell phone and wrecked it. He
Disappeared then,
Wasn't heard from again—
We think that he went to Schenectady.

I promised the director of my daughter's school that I'd write one for her and it wasn't Poughkeepsie, in which case she'd be a gypsy, no, it was a puzzler.

Our director Jenn Scully from Syracuse
Is sad that her near and her dear accuse
Her of practicality
And sense of reality
Rather than more atmospheric views.

Not to toot my own horn, but it is, hands down, the best Syracuse limerick ever written. The envious see it and think, "I have better things to do with my life than spend an hour coming up with the *Syracuse/dear accuse/atmospheric views* rhymes. I have a family." Well, it didn't take me an hour. It came to me in an instant as I stood outside Miss Scully's office door waiting to go in to hear about Maia's achievements in school.

While you aim for the Schenectady and Syracuse limericks, of course you do not decline to pick the low-hanging fruit.

A young man from Oklahoma
Thought that he had carcinoma.
He got in his car,
Drove to the ER,
They said, "No, it's just your aroma."

A Baptist girl from Tucson
Wore a see-through dress of chiffon
In a bright shade of red
And the things that it said
Are not found in the Gospel of John.

141

A lady of east Tennessee
Once thought she was in love with me
But when she caught sight
Of me in daylight
She walked away ASAP.

A lady of north Arkansas
Was in love with me until her pa
Googled my name
And found I was fam-
Ous for walking around in the raw.

As you can see, if you weren't already aware, the limerick tends to be about shame, defeat, and rejection. But not inevitably. When I flew to Manchester, New Hampshire, to give a speech to the journalism school about the First Amendment, it struck me on the way that anyone can give a talk about Freedom of the Press, but how many people can rhyme *Manchester* and which of the two will give more pleasure to an audience of students?

I'm thrilled to be in Manchester
Where all sorts of intense romances stir.
Up in New Hampshire
You can be damn sure
You will soon become someone's ancestor.

Their motto is "Live free or die"
And so they're always sky-high
And vulgar and loud,
With heads unbowed
To any restrictions, no lie.

The men are loose as can be
The women are wild and free,
And even the nuns

Have sinned at least once
And Lutherans, occasionally.

The students were stunned. I went on to address the First but it would've been more memorable if I'd simply said:

The Amendment we know as the First
Protects the *Times, Post,* and Hearst
Who report what is true
But it doesn't help you
When you yelled at your sweetheart and cursed.

New England names are hard—Stonington, Cambridge, Rutland, Marlborough—though I did come up with:

A barber who lived in Connecticut
Regardless of whose patron's head he cut
Picked up his shears
And cut off their ears,
A grave violation of etiquette.

An old fellow lived in Two Harbors
Who never patronized barbers.
He let his hair grow
Ten feet or so,
Which he wore on overhead arbors.

I like the anonymity of the limerick. Anon is fine by me. I never said my name on *A Prairie Home Companion.* I loved writing "Talk of the Town" pieces for *The New Yorker* back when they were unsigned. What did it matter who wrote "Hoppers," a piece about the various styles of people leaping over big puddles in the gutters of Midtown Manhattan on a rainy day? Anonymity helped stifle lit'ry self-consciousness. I quit the magazine when a new editor came in who was all about celebrity and buzz. I knew the power of celebrity, of course, I could see the excitement of the *Prairie*

Home staff when a famous performer appeared, but as a Minnesotan, I resisted it, too. People should be judged by what they do, not by who they know. The St. Paul blues harmonica guy Tony Glover was a great musician but when the newspaper wrote about him, the only way they could suggest his greatness was to mention that Dylan respected him and so did Mick Jagger. Name-dropping as certification. Now and then people asked why we didn't have Dylan on the show. Because I don't care to be associated with him, that's why.

> There is a songwriter named Bob
> Who makes some people's hearts throb.
> They find a thrill in
> Listening to Dylan,
> And for me it's more like a job.

I think that "My Back Pages" is one of the worst songs ever written. I could name others. It's no wonder he took a pseudonym, so as to avoid bringing shame on the Zimmerman family. Myself, I enjoy anonymity. One more reason to write limericks.

> New York. I'm a famous guy there.
> I know because people don't stare.
> They look and they blink,
> Look away and they think,
> "It's him. Yes, it is. Over there."

> I walk along Central Park West
> And passersby all do their best
> To respect privacy
> And not stare at me
> And nobody does. I'm impressed.

> Then I think, "Wait! Could it be
> They really don't recognize me?"
> Now I wear dark glasses

And when someone passes,
I duck my head so they can't see.

And these days I seldom leave home.
I live in a small twilight zone.
I'm sure people mention
My lack of attention:
I'm famous for being unknown.

Limericks are the only poems passed on orally, often by men in road-houses. Russ may tell Mick the one about the young fellow from Pocatello, but he is unlikely to mention my name, even if he knows it. That's all right by me. I go on writing them for the pleasure of it. Most writing— face it—you don't honestly know as you write if it's good or not; you hope so but you've been wrong in the past. I look at pieces of mine that were chosen for anthologies of *New Yorker* humor and they're roadkill. It's embarrassing. I don't listen to my CDs ever. Don't read reviews, especially not the good ones.

I am wary of honors and prizes. It's a Minnesota thing. Back in the Eighties, I got invited to speak at colleges around Minnesota, especially church schools, due, I suppose, to the fact that I often sang gospel songs on the radio and I told stories about the Lutherans and Catholics of Lake Wobegon. I was glad to go, I never accepted a fee, the people were kind, but I felt uneasy about the deference shown to me, as if I were wearing holy cologne. It dawned on me slowly that I had become Famous in Minnesota, at least among My Kind of People, and this disturbed me. I'm a Minnesotan: I was brought up to Fit In, not Stand Out. To a Christian, it feels weird to be praised for my beliefs; it gave me a case of the yips. And that's how I came to write these dirty limericks about good people to preserve myself from sanctimony and the sin of pride. Sometimes I wrote them as I sat onstage about to be introduced by a professor or dean who would talk about his great pride at being in my company. Writing a dirty limerick about the school felt like a fundamentally healthy thing to do.

Luther College stands in Decorah,
Far from Sodom, far from Gomorrah.
Where students are liable
To carry a Bible,
Which they read by the light of their aura.

There's a famous choir at St. Olaf,
Which Lutheran truth is the soul of.
And to sing a hymn and
Sit near the women
A Lutheran man feels is the goal of.

A girl from St. Olaf, an Ole,
Smeared herself with guacamole
And two theologians
Put on their Trojans
And had her, completely and wholly.

A sweet young woman at Bethel
Got a note from her grandmother Ethel:
"Screw boys to death
But stay off of meth,
Sex will not kill you but meth'll."

Good Catholic boys of St. Thomas,
When they matriculate, promise
To avoid romance,
Never unzip their pants,
And marry girls just like their mamas.

At the College of St. Scholastica,
Morals are rather elastic, a
Girl might think, "Cop-
Ulation? No! Stop!"
And the next day, "Molto fantastica!"

At Holy Angels Academy,
They point out the sin of Adam, he
Glanced at her bust
And experienced lust
So they do not teach female anatomy.

They tell of a girl at Concordia
Who likes to come running toward ya
And tear off her clothes,
Stand nose to nose,
And then carefully climb up aboard ya.

The good Lutherans at Augsburg U
Make sure they're unable to screw
By donning a pair
Of steel underwear
That is fastened with C-clamps and glue.

The Catholic girls of St. Ben's
See life through a sanctified lens.
But at twenty-one
They whoop and they run,
Drop the robes and jump over the fence.
Four years of church in
Search of the Virgin
And the urge to emerge is immense.

The Catholic girls of St. Kate's
Are happy to go out on dates
But only for dinner
And to talk about inner
Feelings in mystical states
With a man who is pure
And who, she is sure,
Feels guilty when he masturbates.

The Lutheran boys of Gustavus
Pray, "O Lord who forgave us
Our sexual thoughts,
If we get the hots
For a Catholic woman, Lord, save us."

At United Theological Seminary,
The students are high-minded (very)
And there is no mission-
Ary position
Before the first anniversary.

I was proud of these limericks, especially the St. Kate's and Bethel ones, and I've been waiting decades to publish them, knowing that when I do, I will never be invited to any of these schools ever again, which I very much regret, but art comes with a price, and great art comes with a higher price. They don't teach you that in school but it's true.

22

There Is an Old Man
So Obsessed

With limericks, he simply can't rest
On his laurels, but quickly
(For laurels are prickly)
The pen to the paper is pressed.

I KNOW A WOMAN on Facebook named Hailey—a fiftyish woman stuck in adolescence, who writes the worst verse ever and posts it daily.

I look at my fingertips.
This is me. The only me
Who will ever exist. Made
Of sunsets, birch trees, and summer
Thunderstorms. I
Am a child of God,
Made in Her image
And She in mine.

People leave comments: "This is so beautiful" and "May I share this with others?" and "You have just made my day." Nobody writes, "I hope you are the only you because there is enough horseshit in the world as it is."

There is a winding dirt road off the main highway.
I have passed it many times.
Today I plan to stop and see where it goes.
Otherwise I will always wish I had.

Limericism saved me from writing the Winding Dirt Road poem, if I had tendencies in that direction, which—who knows?—if I drank enough Merlot while staring into a fire, I might. Instead, I carry scrap paper and a pen and while I'm waiting for my jeans to dry or the toast to pop, I allow the limerick to come to me.

The dryer goes round on high spin
With my old blue jeans locked within
And the cycle stops
Just as the toast pops
And hot coffee runs down my chin.

I went for years without writing limericks because I was eager to be successful, to write novels about which a *Times* reviewer would say "beneath the antic brilliance is a piercing, almost Kafkaesque, intelligence that goes straight to the heart of the human dilemma" and this would keep my name in print, meanwhile I'd make the radio show as good as it could be, and then I turned 70 and all of that ambition petered out and I faced up to the fact of boredom. Television bores me and so do parties and dinners except for a few and so do nine-tenths of all lectures and speeches. In the time I've spent trapped in a seat, I could've written *War and Peace*. Too bad it's already been written.

My mother didn't believe in boredom or other forms of melancholy. She said, "There is nothing special about feeling bad. Nobody needs to hear about it." Her cure for boredom was: go outdoors and do something useful; mow the lawn. So I did and found lawn mowing very satisfying: the repetitiveness, the roar of the mower, the sense of progress, turning raggedy grass into an even plane. An hour of mowing and my misery had dissipated. I get the same relief now from writing limericks.

I sit in the little auditorium for my great-nephew's graduation from the program for learning-challenged children of financially gifted parents and the speaker heads down the old *Learning Is a Lifetime Proposition* road and I take out paper and pencil.

> The commencement speaker is speaking
> Like a gas valve quietly leaking
> As every eye closes
> And the audience dozes,
> The clichés groaning and creaking.

> There in his flowing black gown
> With a solemn avuncular frown,
> He instructs and advises
> And the crowd fantasizes
> About a truck running him down.

I ride a bus and it inches along through heavy traffic and passes a hospital and a young man in blue scrubs gets off, and we sit at a red light, and everyone on the bus is bored silly except me, the man with pen and paper.

> There was a young hospital clerk
> Who rode the bus daily to work.
> On buses he's ridden, he's
> Stolen folks' kidneys
> And sold them for transplants, the jerk.

It's ridiculous to devote myself to a childish genre, the limerick. I am well aware of this. Other people do nobler things with their lives. I once met the daughter of a Japanese linguist who devoted twenty years of his life to creating a dictionary for the Nez Perce Indians, who had never had a written language. This patient, saintly man went to Idaho and listened to the elders talk and transcribed their words into phonetic symbols and organized them, with definitions, into a practical tool to preserve the language into the future. He himself could speak Nez Perce, but with a

Japanese accent, which he did not want the Nez Perce to pick up, so he mainly sat still and listened and took notes. The Nez Perce young were being bombarded by radio, TV, movies, pop music, the internet, while this old man, who went to college in Hiroshima before it was devastated, sat and pieced together a grammar of their ancestral tongue. This strikes me as nobility of a very high order.

> A scholarly man from Japan
> Made a grand linguistic plan
> For the Nez Perce,
> Chapter and verse,
> If they wish to speak, so they can.

My cousin Alec Johnson, an astrophysicist, did similar work in behalf of impoverished people in northern Uganda, raising money to dig wells and build schools and send young people to college to learn sustainable agriculture.

> A good man was Doctor A. J.
> Who traveled far out of his way
> To arid Uganda
> To build a school and a
> Hostel in which students stay.
>
> An astrophysicist, he
> Was acquainted with gravity.
> Did all he could do
> To fly and he flew
> Nearer, Uganda, to thee.

My nephew Douglas has done heroic work in behalf of public school teachers, my niece Kristina as a speech therapist for veterans suffering from PTSD, whereas I am the author of *She bent and her décolletage appeared as a golden mirage*. The contrast is not lost on me. My grandmother prayed I'd be a teacher, as did my aunt Eleanor, while Mother thought I had a gift for preaching. But I had no patience for the ignorant, which everyone is until they get taught, and I knew too much about lust and pride to be a preacher. So I settled into a life of *scribblescribble* and practiced niceness rather than virtue.

> I am ashamed of me, truly,
> For loving limericks unduly
> And preferring hilarity
> To deeds of charity
> But at least I'm not wild and unruly.
> Ask Karen. Ask Shirley or Julie.
> I never scratched
> Or bit or snatched
> Their scarves or treated them cruelly.

I was elected to the American Academy of Arts and Letters in 2001 because I read poems on the radio every day on *The Writer's Almanac* and so got the votes of poets. It was not then widely known that I wrote limericks. Fifteen years later, for the May ceremonial, I was invited to give the Blashford Address, following in the footsteps of William Crary Brownell (*The Academy and the Language*), A. Whitney Griswold (*Further Obsequies for the Grammarian*), J. William Fulbright (*Our Foreign Policy*), Aldous Huxley (*Utopias, Positive and Negative*), Henry Steele Commager (*Recreating the Community of Culture*), Henry Louis Gates, Jr. (*Matthew Arnold and Multiculturalism*). My address was *My Legacy, The Limerick* and it was met with painful silence. The address came after a cocktail hour and a lunch, and I was aware of heavy breathing in the background. I had written limericks about a number of members including:

> For the sage humorist Calvin Trillin,
> Kansas City is where his heart's still in,
> A town where Blue Cross
> Pays for barbecue sauce
> As a drug along with penicillin.

When you meet a writer named Prose,
You expect her to plow in straight rows
But when she's Francine
You see it might mean
She farms in elegant clothes.

Here is to Angell, old Rog,
The dean of the sportswriters' lodge,
Who remembers the Giants
And knuckleball science
And the Dodgers before they left Dodge.

A writer of prose, Janet Malcolm,
Makes paragraphs dusted with talcolm,
Dry, aromatic,
Lyric, emphatic—
"Thanks," I say. She says, "You're walcolm."

A lady who'd read Don DeLillo
Lay her head down on a pillow
And dreamed about Dallas,
Dystopian malice,
And danced with a dark armadillo.

The applause that followed was just enough to cover me turning and walking four steps to my seat and sitting down. Afterward, people avoided making eye contact.

The Academy of Arts and Letters
Is a kennel of old Irish setters,
Each one pedigreed
As the best of their breed,
Plus a few of us shrewd counterfeiters.

We sit in our A&L sweaters,

Editors, creditors, debtors.

I try my hardest

To look like an artist,

Worried and wan,

Quite woebegone,

But clearly I'm one,

When all's said and done,

Who was good running big manure spreaders.

✤ **23** ✤

Weaponization

I BELIEVE IN the limerick of friendship, but of course I'm only human and sometimes a person needs to pick up manure and throw it at a sacred cow.

> Carl Sandburg wrote hagiography
> As flat as Midwest geography.
> When Lincoln was shot,
> He was glad he would not
> Have to read the Sandburg biography.

It occurred to me that nobody had given Proust a poke in the snoot for a long time and maybe it's up to me to supply one. A short, sharp poke, not a Proustian one.

> The great novelist Marcel Proust
> Wrote lengthy tomes to be used
> To keep a door shut
> Or place under a butt
> To give a short person a boost.
>
> His *Remembrance of Everything Past*
> Is not a book you hold fast
> And cling to your heart,

156

Reluctant to part,
Hoping the flavor will last.

And so the practical French,
Using a hammer and wrench,
Found it easy to glue
Together a few
And make a table or bench.

My campaign against the Swedish Academy, which gives out the Nobel in Literature every year to a dullard, has been fruitless.

Whoever gives out the Nobel
Literature Prize, go to hell
And there you will find
Men of like mind
Who cannot feel, touch, hear, or smell.

Bleak, enigmatic, pretentious,
The Swedes sit on hard wooden benches
Like funeral clerks
And honor the works
That soon will be buried in trenches.

What's wrong with humorous, Sven?
Why dismal again and again?
Lighten up, Ole,
Lightness is holy.
Blest is the comic. Amen.

I struck a slight glancing blow at *The Elements of Style*, the bible of English usage carried by every college freshman. A fine book. And yet—

The manual by Strunk & White
Can teach you to write nice and tight
Little prose pieces,

No wrinkles, no creases,
A thesis that's neat and polite.

Sometimes I think White & Strunk
Were really a Catholic monk
And that for style
They should dance for a while
With a girl who's outstandingly drunk.

In other words, lighten up, guys.
Remove the loupe from your eyes.
Loosen your undies
On Tuesdays and Sundays,
And improvise, boys, improvise.

And then there was a heroine of American art whose leafy work was everywhere for a while.

Georgia O'Keeffe painted flowers
But once, after two vodka sours,
She painted a wiener,
A gross misdemeanor,
And was jailed for a couple of hours.

A woman once wrote an essay for *Time Magazine* titled "Let's Leave Garrison Keillor in the Past Where He Belongs," which I admired for its all-out animus. I had done her the favor of releasing all the anger she had stored up against Hitler, Stalin, Genghis Khan, and perhaps some men she had known personally. The gist of her essay was: you're old, sit down, shut up, go away, you make me sick, boogers on you, please die. No woman had done me the honor of despising me so thoroughly since I was in the third grade. So I wrote her a limerick:

A millennial named McInerny
Is my prosecuting attorney

And recommends death
With fiery breath,
A stack of indictments on her knee.

I'm in awe of your venom, dear Nora,
But not yet pushing up flora.
And the mist round your head
As you wish me dead
Is aroma, my dear, not an aura.
I like your cigar
As you stand at the bar,
Your ferocious grin as you pour a
Jigger of gin
And the diamond stickpin
In the barbed wire on your fedora.

In Richmond, back at a time when people in the audience would stand up in reverence if the band played "Dixie," I did:

The Confederate general Bob E. Lee
Committed treason quite freely
And General Grant
Beat him up 'cause you can't
Attack federal troops—I mean *really.*

No need to give a speech: five lines was enough. He fought hard in a bad cause. It's happened to many a good man. It's too bad that he was such a brilliant general that he managed to prolong the war two or three years and cause even more death and destruction. But I'm sure he thought about that after Appomattox.

The limerick of derision is very satisfying, and in 2000, we saw an election swiped in broad daylight by nine justices in black robes and what's to be done about it? Nothing. So why not at least have the pleasure of writing a limerick.

A good Democrat named Al Gore
Lost the battle though he'd won the war
When old Karl Rove
Stole the pies from the stove—
And look at who walked through the door—
President Bush's son George
Who campaigned on his front porch,
Giving wedgies and hickeys
And drinking gin rickeys
And lighting his farts with a torch.
The Supreme Court, son of a gun,
Stopped the count and he won,
And we liberals for days
Wrote thoughtful essays
On our deep sense of deprivation.

Anger is fuel, and without it we'd be dozing face-first into the potato salad. Today I read about the righteous lefties on college campuses and am grateful I went to school in a looser, more freewheeling time.

The students of Mount Holyoke
Think hard before telling a joke:
Might it disturb,
Diminish, perturb,
Marginalize or provoke,
Make one feel harassed?
Then the moment is past
When the comment could have been spoke.

A man should avoid Middlebury
Unless he is quite sanitary
And holds no views
That might loosen the screws
Of the student constabulary.

To be at Harvard or Yale
As a white Anglo humorous male
Is fatal. Surrender,
Question your gender,
Be liquid, find trauma, travail.
Write a memoir
On how you are
In pain: here's a hammer and nail.

In 2016, when the Unthinkable became the Inevitable and a New York real-estate thug, the epitome of the Ugly American, was elected president and the country went into shell shock, it was no time to be polite. The Republican Party gave us an incompetent narcissist, a charlatan with less fidelity to factual truth than any real-estate developer in America, and he is enabled by cynical and dishonest men.

McConnell the senator, Mitch,
Is an ugly old son of a bitch,
A man with no chin
Who puts the fix in
Every day for the filthily rich.

The soft-spoken Senator Graham
Addresses Herr Trump as Te Deum.
He talks Suthin,
Does he know nothin'
Or did the president pay him?

The caustic Senator Cruz
Avoids media interviews:
One look at his smirk
On a TV network,
And folks of both sexes
All over Texas,

The reds as well as the blues,
Devoutly pray he will lose.

Senator Collins of Maine
Runs a brilliant campaign
Every six years,
The lady appears
To be calm and reasonably sane.
And otherwise
She covers her eyes
And votes from the back of her brain
With the elephants all in a train.

As for the man himself, he is unspeakable. My good Christian relatives who love him struck a bargain with the devil and what can you say to people who look at the emperor in his transparent underwear and see those little things and imagine it's jewelry?

Dear Mr. Trump, Donald J.,
We are praying that you go away.
Paraguay or Peru,
Any country will do
So long as it's far and you stay.

You said the swamp would be drained,
Were elected, and that day it rained
And the sharks who were waiting
Began masturbating
And the gators were well-entertained.

If the bankers said, *Hop,* you would jump.
On history's log, you're a bump.
You're no Andrew Jackson,
Just an old Anglo-Saxon,
With a gut, bad hair, and big rump.

Your only true friend is Sean Hannity,
Propelled by the gases of vanity,
And with great gravity
From his oral cavity,
Come clouds of vicious insanity.

You're a faker, a wuss, and a weenie.
Your hands are sweaty and teeny.
You're a joke. It's so sad.
Your ratings are bad.
You're crookeder than fettuccine.

You're the air in a blank envelope.
You can lie, you can rant, you can grope.
You will be impeached
When the limit is reached
Which should be next week, one would hope.

And with impeachment in the air and ambitious lawyers circling, what about the quiet little man who carries the Big Man's coat?

The smiling Vice President Pence
Should think up his legal defense:
Was his phone lost?
Were his fingers crossed?
Is he deaf or blind?
Was he out of his mind
Or just, as we used to say, "dense"?

But the shelf life of fools is terribly brief. Demagoguery is a fly-by-night business. Father Coughlin, Fulton Lewis Jr., Joe McCarthy, the incendiaries of my youth, are gone and forgotten; a limerick about any of them would be dead on arrival.

A limerick against Franklin Pierce
And the dead matter between his ears

163

Might feel pretty great
In 1858
But less so in more recent years.

Likewise the sharp limerick shaft
Aimed at McKinley or Taft
Was fine for a while
And made people smile
But it's been years since anyone laughed.

At a party for my nephew's French girlfriend, Kate, I discovered, speaking of the Boy President, that she does not understand the English words "corrupt," "mendacious," "bully," though she does know "dishonest" (*malhonnête*). The word "mendacious" is not useful in love nor in her line of work, which is engineering: it leads to nothing. So I wrote her a limerick.

A young French woman named Kate
Came into our family late
And brought savoir-faire
And amour, mon cher,
And made our Matt a good mate.

Which reminded me of a girl named Cathy whom I danced with when I was fifteen. She wasn't a Kate and she didn't actually kiss me and I'm only seventy-seven, but the memory is so sweet, I had to bend it a little.

Here's to my classmate dear Kate
Who kissed me once on a date
Back in ninth grade
And the memory stayed
With me decades—I'm seventy-eight!

In other words, life goes on.

🌿 24 🌿

Freddy Keillor, 2000–2017

SMALL SORROWS SPEAK; great sorrows are silent. Limericks have always addressed small sorrows —*There was an old man of St. Paul who was always depressed in the fall*—*There was a young man of Minneapolis who lost GPS and was mapless*—but a writer tries to extend the reach of the genre. Limericks about death are about a silly death, like the old lady named Liz who choked to death on Cheez Whiz, or the boy who was not so bright and lit a candle one night, then saw 'twas no wick but the fuse of a stick of his father's best dynamite. My grandson Frederick died accidentally in his bedroom while experimenting with a length of rope. He was curious about thousands of things, death definitely not one of them, and his experiment went crazy wrong, blighting the lives of his mother and brother and father and all of us who loved him and who had patiently listened to him over the years telling us about cars, stars, planets, and everything else he had been reading about. This boy so loving and eager is gone and the vacancy gets deeper as time goes by and the possibility of who he might be grows larger.

> My grandson Frederick, young Freddy,
> Was a comer, kept pressing ahead, he
> Studied Chinese,

Knew hundreds of trees,
He tossed out facts like confetti.

He knew everything about cars,
The bugs he collected in jars,
The various merits
Of foxes and ferrets,
The constellations of stars.

He never meant, God forbid,
To cause the grief that he did,
But perhaps to go high
And fly to the sky
And return as a more starstruck kid.

We think of him out there at play
As the light is fading away.
Though he is dead, he
Forever is Freddy,
Still in existence
Though at a distance,
Turning and learning
All things concerning
Ideas, wisdom,
The shape of a system,
Books and articles,
Planets and particles,
Taking delight
In hearing and sight,
Constantly keen
Forever seventeen,
We were lucky to have him, I say.

❧ 25 ❧

The Old Man

SEVENTY-SEVEN IS A good age to devote oneself to the limerick. Sonnets are for winning a woman's heart and I already did that; she's in the next room, reading *Anna Karenina*, drinking a Sauvignon Blanc. I have no urge to write lamentatious poetry—*The sky like dirty laundry hangs over the backyards of St. Paul: why are we here? What are we waiting for?*—Nobody cares about the sorrows of an old man. I don't so why should you? Old age itself is humorous: you stick the word "old" in the first line of a limerick, you've added 35 percent to the humor quotient.

> There was an old man of Nevada
> Who dated a girl and he had a
> Nice time with Nancy
> Till she tickled his fancy
> And he lost control of his bladda.

It's an adventurous age. You walk across ice, you hold out your arms for balance, you know you could slip and hit your head and suddenly your command of the subjunctive mood is gone. So don't fall. Lift your feet lest you become past tense. Drink more water.

> There was an old man of Bay Ridge
> Who cried out, "Son of a bitch.

167

I got up in the night
And on came the light
And I find I have pissed in the fridge."

There was an old man in St. Paul
Put his desk in a Men's toilet stall.
It was quiet, conducive,
And one had the use of
The plumbing, no waiting at all.

At seventy-seven, I regret the time I've wasted, acres of time, in my twenties and thirties, hanging out, watching TV, shooting pool, sitting through laconic Sunday dinners, hours of shopping for clothes in hopes of becoming distinguished—now I have a uniform, jeans and black T-shirt, to save time. No TV for thirty years. The hours are too precious. I don't regret dishwashing or lawn mowing, both ruminative activities. But I regret golf. What was I thinking? Lawyers and bankers play golf and when you think of the damage they would do if they were at the job instead, you realize why golf courses are a wise investment for any municipality.

I have just wrapped my old No. 3
Iron around a pine tree
Where I shanked the drive
But I shall survive
And go write a brief elegy.

Farewell to life on the links!
The game is over! It stinks!
The great plaid butts
Bending over the putts,
The hike to the clubhouse for drinks.

Instead I will write at my desk
Limericks, cool, humoresque,
And if I need dough

I'll go do a show,
Either radio or strip burlesque.

And I regret all the afternoons I've spent aboard somebody's big expensive motorboat.

I once knew a man with a boat.
It was his quote dream unquote.
He was a lawyer
Who loved his destroyer,
The majestic wake
It made on the lake,
The horsepower roar.
I'll go there no more.
Goodbye. I'm gone. That's all I wrote.

I have no regrets about being old, however. To look back to my youth, when Uncle Jim plowed with horses and Grandma lit kerosene lamps, when the phone was in a wooden box on the wall and you turned a crank to get the operator on the line who connected you unless a neighbor was on the line in which case you might listen in, or not. There was no caller ID because only people you knew would call you. We threw our dirty clothes in a washing machine, ran them through a wringer, and hung them out on a clothesline. In hot weather, we put a fan in the bedroom window. I know all about this.

This was before credit cards, even before pizza and LPs, before photocopying. You could put me in a glass case at the historical society and schoolchildren could press a button and ask me questions.

At seventy-seven, one would think, a man would be brooding about his mortality, but I did that in my twenties, and don't need to do it all over again.

Where do we go when we die?
I'm planning on heaven, no lie.
But first I suppose
I must decompose

And be reduced to nuclei,

When hopefully

My spirit gets free

Of this debris and can fly

To join my Maker

At his trillion-acre

Bakery up in the sky.

I will order a chocolate éclair,

A cheese Danish of Camembert,

And, Lord be praised,

Two doughnuts glazed—

When the rolls are called up yonder I'll be there.

26

Postlude

IT WAS CONVULSIVE laughter that drew me into the force field of the limerick, but I'm too old for that now, the snot coming out my nose during *There was a young man of Antietam who loved horse turds so well he could eat 'em. He would sit on their rumps and swallow the lumps as fast as the beasts could excrete 'em.* I look at that now as I'd look at a lab specimen, a dissected frog. *The young man of Madras* used to kill me and the young man of Kent *whose cock was so long that it bent so to save him the trouble he put it in double and instead of coming he went* was hilarious once and now it's history. What I admire about limericks now is mainly the concision.

> A devout young vegan named Sue
> Picked up a sandwich to chew.
> She took a bite
> And cried out in fright,
> "OMG, WTF, BBQ!"

A few of my verses, perhaps Pocatello or the young man who answered an ad or the liberal lady of D.C., may find their way someday into *The Popular Mechanics Anthology of Shorter Verse*, attributed to Anon, and maybe some boy will read them and cut loose with a big whinny of a laugh. That, along with my 1987 rendition of "Joy, Joy, Joy" with Kate MacKenzie and Stevie

Beck and Doc Watson on YouTube and a Guy Noir bobblehead will be my gift to the world. As we say in Minnesota, "Okay, then."

In 2018, my wife and I moved from a three-story six-bedroom seven-bathroom manse in St. Paul to a two-bedroom apartment in Minneapolis, shedding ourselves of truckloads of material goods, so that we could enjoy the gift to be simple and the gift to be free. It had dawned on us that we were two people living in a few corners of a house for ten. We went for hours, sometimes days, without running into each other. We feared that the county would send social workers who specialize in dementia issues. And we longed to move up in the world. Minneapolis is the home of the Guthrie Theater, Walker Art Center, the Institute of Art, and four-fifths of all restaurants where dinner entrees start at $24 and go way up from there, a city often referred to as the Paris of the Midwest. St. Paul is the home of Mickey's Diner, Candyland, the farm campus of the University, and a minor league ball club whose mascot is a pig.

In our little apartment, I have a writing desk in the corner of the guest bedroom and that's where I work. My wife is a few steps away in the living room or else she's practicing the viola in the bedroom. I feel lighter, more agile. On the desk is a jar full of pens and a stack of 5-by-7 paper and a wastebasket. Give me a 5-by-7 sheet of paper and a Pilot rollerball pen and I will write a few lines and see if something good happens.

> Limericks are works of slight craft,
> Tending to be slightly daft,
> And their success
> One only can guess
> By the fact that somebody laughed.

> The limerick is a poetic form
> Beloved by the boys in the dorm
> To whom it will mean
> More if obscene,
> Throbbing and swollen and warm.

This limerick, I'm sorry, is not.
It contains not one filthy thought.
You can read it, my dear,
Without any fear
Of embarrassment should you be caught.

For now that I'm older, the ribald
Seems emotionally crippled,
Though I like the raw
That shocks the bourgeois,
The best has already been scribbled.

There won't be another Nantucket.
That was a huge golden nugget
Of outstanding merits
And hundreds of carats
That belongs to the fellow who struck it.

So a limericist of today
Of necessity makes his own way
And writes for the pleasure
Of taking the measure
Of five lines: A A B B A.

I write of noteworthy occasions,
Of virtues like kindness and patience,
And seldom of farts
And bodily parts,
And remarkable sexual relations.

The bourgeois's not easily shocked.
All of the talk has been talked.
Nothing is sacred,
Everyone's naked,
All of the priests are defrocked.

But wait—she's turned off the shower.
She appears, my darling, my flower.
I hear her howl,
"Where is a towel?"
And here is my lover,
My beauty, all of her—
For a minute. I wish for an hour.

Epilogue

And now I have come to the end.
I hope you enjoyed it, my friend.
I will write more
Until I'm 94
And I'll wave as I go round the bend.

God is good but the workers are few:
A dark world with so much to do.
My job is humor,
Dispelling the rumor
We're alone. We're not: we are two.
You have my heart.
Let us not part.
Did I just fart? Or did you?